ENTERPRISE
GRAMMAR 3

Student's Book

Virginia Evans
Jenny Dooley

Express Publishing

Published by Express Publishing

Liberty House, Greenham Business Park, Newbury,
Berkshire RG19 6HW
Tel: (0044) 1635 817 363
Fax: (0044) 1635 817 463
e-mail: inquiries@expresspublishing.co.uk
http: //www.expresspublishing.co.uk

ISBN 978-1-903128-77-0

Contents

Present Simple

Affirmative	Negative
I work You work He work**s** She work**s** It work**s** We work You work They work	I **don't** work You don't work He **doesn't** work, etc.
	Interrogative
	Do I work? Do you work? **Does** he work? etc.

Short answers

Do I/you, etc. work ...?	Yes, I/you, etc. do. No, I/you, etc. don't.
Does he/she, etc. work ...?	Yes, he/she, etc. does. No, he/she, etc. doesn't.

Use

We use **the present simple** for:
- permanent states, repeated actions and daily routines.
  *Carlos **lives** in Lisbon. (permanent state)*
  *He **goes** to work by bus. (repeated action)*
  *She **gets up** at six o'clock every morning. (daily routine)*
- scheduled actions, i.e. timetables of trains, buses, etc. or programmes.
  *The train to Istanbul **leaves** at 9.00 pm.*
- likes and dislikes.
  *He **likes** horses.*
- general truths or laws of nature.
  *The sun **rises** in the east.*

Time Expressions we use with the present simple:

always, usually, often, etc., **every day/week/ month/year,** etc., **on Mondays/Tuesdays,** etc., **in the morning/afternoon/evening, at night/the weekend,** etc.

Present Continuous

Affirmative	Negative
I **am** work**ing** You are working He is working She is working It is working We are working You are working They are working	I'm not working You aren't working He isn't working, etc.
	Interrogative
	Am I working? Are you working? Is he working? etc.

Short answers

Are you/we, etc. working?	Yes, I am/we are, etc. No, I'm not/we aren't, etc.
Is he/she, etc. working?	Yes, he/she, etc. is. No, he/she, etc. isn't.

Use

We use **the present continuous** for:
- actions happening now, at the moment of speaking.
  *The children **are sleeping** right now.*
- temporary actions, i.e. actions happening around the time of speaking.
  *The Greens **are looking** for a babysitter at the moment.*
- actions that we have already arranged to do in the near future, especially when the time and place have been decided.
  *They**'re flying** to Canada at seven o'clock this evening.*

Time Expressions we use with the present continuous:

now, at the moment, these days, at present, nowadays, still, etc.

State Verbs

- State verbs are verbs which do not normally have continuous tenses because they describe a state rather than an action. These include:

- **verbs expressing likes and dislikes:** like, love, hate, dislike, can't stand, don't mind, prefer, enjoy, etc.
  *Thomas **likes** jazz music.*
  Note: Verbs expressing likes/dislikes take a **noun** or an **-ing form** after them.
          *She **can't stand cats**.*
          *He **loves playing** basketball.*

- **verbs of perception:** believe, know, notice, remember, forget, understand, think, etc.
  *I **don't understand** the meaning of that word.*

- **verbs of the senses:** see, hear, feel, taste, look, smell, sound. We often use **can** or **could** with these verbs when we refer to what we see, hear, etc., at the moment of speaking.
  *The cake **tastes** delicious.*
  *I can **hear** children's voices coming from the playground.*

- **some other verbs:** fit, contain, need, belong, cost, owe, mean, own, appear, want, have (= possess), etc.
  *This dress is very expensive. It **costs** £250.*
  Some state verbs have continuous tenses, but there is a difference in meaning.

  1) *I **think** she needs help. (= I believe ...)*
     *I'm **thinking about** buying a new car. (= I'm considering ...)*

  2) *This pasta **tastes** delicious! (= This pasta has a delicious flavour.)*
     *He's **tasting** the pasta. (= He's testing the flavour of ...)*

  3) *I can **see** a light in the distance. (= I can actually see ...)*
     *I'm **seeing** Tom this evening. (= I'm meeting ...)*

  4) *George **looks** very tired. (= George appears to be ...)*
     *John **is looking** at an old map. (= John is studying ...)*

  5) *The kitchen always **smells** of freshly baked bread. (= The kitchen always has the smell of ...)*
     *Why **is** the lady **smelling** the perfume? (= Why is the lady sniffing ...)*

  6) *This material **feels** soft. (= This material has a soft texture ...)*
     *A: Why **are** you **feeling** Sam's forehead? (= Why are you touching ...)*
     B: Because I think he's got a temperature.

  7) *She **has** a beautiful old house. (= She owns/possesses ...)*
     *We **are having** dinner. (= We are eating ...)*

Linking Words/Phrases

- To join similar ideas or add more points we can use **and (also)**, **also** or **and ... as well**.
  *He's got brown hair **and** brown eyes. He's **also** got full lips.*
  *She is polite **and (also)** generous.*
  *She is polite **and** generous **as well**.*

- To join contrasting ideas or facts we can use **but**, **however** or **on the other hand**.
  Susan is very generous. She can be a bit bossy.
  *Susan is very generous **but** she can be a bit bossy.*
  *Susan is very generous. **However/On the other hand**, she can be a bit bossy.*

Present Simple - Present Continuous

1 Put the verbs below into the correct box in the 3rd person singular, as in the examples.

forget, express, say, study, take, buy, tidy, eat, drive, crash, play, do, cry, fly, lay, boil, pass, stay, teach, fry

+ s	forgets,
ss, sh, ch, x, o, + es	expresses,
vowel + y + s	says,
consonant + ✗ ➡ ies	studies,

2 Add -ing to the verbs in the list below and put them into the correct box, as in the examples.

draw, lie, dive, put, drink, run, sit, tie, give, apply, live, grow, begin, type, die, repair

+ ing	drawing,
-✗ ➡ y + ing	lying,
✗ ➡ ing	diving,
double consonant + ing	putting,

3 a) Put the verbs in brackets into the correct form of the present simple or present continuous, as in the example.

1 I ...*am flying*... **(fly)** to Moscow tomorrow.
2 The McCarthys .... **(live)** in Perth.
3 John .... **(paint)** the garage at the moment.
4 The earth .... **(move)** around the sun.
5 Anna .... **(like)** her new school.
6 The flight to New York .... **(leave)** at 7:00 am.
7 We .... **(look)** for new furniture for the living room at present.
8 .... **(you/go)** to Spain this summer?
9 Rachel .... **(work)** as a waitress at *Sunrise Diner*.
10 The train from Brussels .... **(arrive)** at 5:10 pm.
11 We .... **(stay)** at a beautiful hotel by the sea.
12 Ellen .... **(hate)** dogs.
13 She .... **(exercise)** three times a week.
14 I .... **(write)** a letter to Michael right now.
15 Water .... **(freeze)** at 0˚C.

b) Which sentences describe:

A	a permanent state	= ...2,...
B	a temporary action	= ....
C	a scheduled action	= ....
D	an action arranged for the near future	= ....
E	a general truth	= ....
F	an action happening now	= ....
G	likes/dislikes	= ....
H	a routine	= ....

4 Underline the correct form of the verb.

1 Stacey **goes/is going** shopping for fruit and vegetables every Saturday morning.
2 He **doesn't speak/isn't speaking** five languages.
3 Bob **drives/is driving** the children to the match tonight.
4 Julie **enjoys/is enjoying** listening to classical music.
5 **Do they play/Are they playing** in the garden at the moment?
6 John and Mary **hate/are hating** adventure holidays.
7 They **look/are looking** for a house to rent.
8 The flight to London **departs/is departing** at 10:05 am.
9 Mrs Parker **teaches/is teaching** History at Lawton High School.
10 Melissa **doesn't like/isn't liking** mini-skirts.
11 Water **boils/is boiling** at 100˚C.
12 What **do you do/are you doing** this Saturday night?

5 Put the verbs in brackets into the correct form of the present simple or present continuous, as in the example.

Dear Philip,
    I **1)** ...*am writing*... **(write)** to tell you about my holiday. I **2)** .....am staying........... **(stay)** with my friend in Spain for two weeks. It **3)** ......is................ **(be)** usually sunny at this time of year, but at the moment it **4)** ...is raining.... **(rain)**. Tomorrow morning we **5)** ...are going to.. **(go)** sightseeing and in the evening we **6)** ...are planning... **(plan)** to go out for a nice meal. We both **7)** ....enjoy...... **(enjoy)** Spanish food very much. I **8)** ...arriving.... **(arrive)** home next Saturday.
    See you then,

                                              Love,
                                              Carol

6 Look at the pictures and use the prompts to write questions and answers in the present simple or the present continuous.

1 what/he/do/every Saturday?
....
....
....

2 she/play tennis/at the moment?
....
....
....

3 Lee/have/a singing lesson?
....
....
....

4 how/Lesley/go to school?
....
....
....

5 Paul and Sue/drink coffee now?
....
....
....

7 Put the verbs in brackets into the correct form of the present simple or present continuous.

1 A: What **1)** .... **(you/cook)**?
    B: I **2)** .... **(make)** vegetarian lasagne.
    A: **3)** .... **(you/eat)** vegetables every day?
    B: No, I usually **4)** .... **(have)** meat at the weekend.

2 A: What **1)** .... **(you/do)** tonight?
    B: Nothing special. Why?
    A: Would you like to go to the cinema?
    B: That **2)** .... **(sound)** like a good idea. What **3)** .... **(you/want)** to see?
    A: I'd really like to see *Titanic*.
    B: I **4)** .... **(hate)** watching sad films.
    A: How about a comedy then?
    B: OK.

3 A: **1)** .... **(you/spend)** the summer in Sicily?
    B: No, this year we **2)** .... **(go)** to the north of Scotland. A friend of ours **3)** .... **(have)** a cottage near Inverness.
    A: Oh, how wonderful! **4)** .... **(you/take)** the children with you?
    B: No, they **5)** .... **(stay)** with my mother because they **6)** .... **(not/like)** being away from their friends.

8 **Put the verbs in brackets into the correct form.**

Bridget **1)** .....goes..... **(go)** to school every morning at 8 o'clock. Right now, she **2)** .....is..... .....sitting..... **(sit)** next to her friend, Sue. Their teacher **3)** ....is talking.... **(talk)** to them about Argentina and they **4)** ...are trying... **(try)** to find it on the globe. Bridget **5)** ......loves...... **(love)** Geography but she **6)** .....hates..... **(hate)** Maths. Every month, the teacher **7)** ....shows.... .....to..... **(show)** the class a film about another country. Bridget really **8)** .....enjoys..... **(enjoy)** these films. In fact, she **9)** ....wants.... **(want)** to be a Geography teacher one day.

9 **Put the verbs in brackets into the correct form of the present simple or the present continuous.**

1 A: **1)** .... **(the baby/sleep)**?
   B: No, she **2)** .... **(not/be)**. She **3)** .... **(play)**.
2 A: Where **1)** .... **(you/go)** on holiday this year?
   B: I **2)** .... **(want)** to go to Spain but my wife **3)** .... **(prefer)** Turkey.
3 A: Hi, Mum. We **1)** .... **(have)** a great time here in Venice.
   B: Oh, lovely. When **2)** .... **(you/come)** home? On Friday?
   A: No, we **3)** .... **(not/be)**. We **4)** .... **(come)** back on Saturday.
4 A: What **1)** .... **(you/usually/have)** for breakfast?
   B: I usually **2)** .... **(have)** tea and toast but sometimes I **3)** .... **(eat)** cereal for a change.
5 A: What **1)** .... **(you/think)** of my new dress? **2)** .... **(you/like)** it?
   B: Yes, I **3)** .... **(do)** . **4)** .... **(you/wear)** it tonight?
   A: No, I **5)** .... **(not/be)**. I **6)** .... **(save)** it for John's party.

Linking Words/Phrases

10 **Underline the correct word(s).**

1 I love coffee **but/as well** I hate tea.
2 Sally is a co-operative **and/also** energetic person.
3 Mike is friendly. **However/As well**, he tends to be arrogant at times.
4 Peter's short, well-built **and/but** middle-aged. He's got curly grey hair and brown eyes **as well/ also**. He's **however/also** got a rather big nose.
5 Pam loves wearing V-neck jumpers **but/and** leggings.
6 Jessica is caring, generous and patient **but/as well**.
7 Ellen likes sharing her toys with other children. **And/On the other hand**, she can be rude at times.
8 Laura is a very hard worker. She's **however/also** an imaginative person.

11 **Read the letter below and underline the correct word(s).**

Dear John,

Thanks for your letter. It sounds like you're enjoying yourself at university. Anyway, here's the recipe for the apple pie that you asked for. It's cheap **1) also/and also** easy to make.

First, you need about ten large cooking apples and some sugar **2) as well/also**. Peel the apples **3) and/ but** cut them into pieces. Then, boil them with the sugar until they are soft. You could make some pastry **4) but/also** ready-made pastry is just as nice. Roll the pastry until it's thin and put it into a greased dish. Put the apples into the dish, too. Sprinkle some cinnamon on top **5) and/also** cover it with more pastry. Put it in the oven at 180°C **6) but/also** don't leave it for too long. I always serve it with fresh cream. **7) On the other hand/But**, it tastes great with ice-cream.

Well, let me know how your exams go **8) and/but** enjoy the apple pie.

Love from
Aunt Jane

12 **Use the words in brackets to write the questions to these statements, as in the example.**

1 Every morning I get up at 7 o'clock. **(What time)**
   ...*What time do you get up every morning?*...
2 They have toast and eggs for breakfast. **(What)**
   ....
3 We like going to the seaside at weekends. **(Where)**
   ....

4 John's brother is 15 years old. (**How old**)

....

5 My father plays golf three times a week. (**How often**)

....

6 I usually shop for groceries on Tuesdays. (**When**)

....

13 **Choose the correct item.**

1 This roast chicken .... delicious!
   A taste   **B** is tasting   **C** tastes

2 They go to the cinema ....
   A every week   **B** at the moment   **C** usually

3 .... you seeing Peter tomorrow night?
   A Do   **B** Are   **C** Is

4 A: Can I help you, miss?
   B: Yes, I .... for a birthday present for my daughter.
   A look   **B** 'm looking   **C** looks

5 .... she wear a uniform at work?
   A Are   **B** Is   **C** Does

6 A: These shirts .... me any more.
   B: Why don't you buy some new ones?
   A doesn't fit   **B** don't fit   **C** isn't fitting

7 I enjoy travelling by train but I .... travelling by plane.
   A like   **B** hate   **C** likes

8 Annette .... two sisters and a brother.
   A has   **B** is having   **C** have

9 A: You .... very pretty today.
   B: Thanks.
   A are looking   **B** look   **C** looks

10 A: When .... she leaving for Boston?
   B: On the 15th of July.
   A does   **B** has   **C** is

11 My brother is a very easy-going person. ...., he can be a bit rude at times.
   A However   **B** As well as   **C** And

12 A: Are you .... anything at the weekend?
   B: No, I'm not.
   A do   **B** does   **C** doing

Error Correction

14 **Cross out the unnecessary word, as in the example.**

1 She ~~is~~ often goes to the park on Sundays.
2 They are been going on holiday on Monday.
3 I am enjoy going to parties.
4 The plane from Paris does arrives at 7.30.
5 They are looking for a house at the present.
6 Does he do listen to music in his free time?
7 I like swimming but I don't like fishing too.
8 She is at home at now.

Word Formation

We can form adjectives from nouns by adding the following suffixes.	
-ous	e.g. fame - fam**ous**
-ive	e.g. aggression - aggress**ive**
-ful	e.g. beauty - beauti**ful**
-y	e.g. boss - boss**y**
-ly	e.g. friend - friend**ly**

15 **Fill in the gaps with the correct words derived from the words in bold.**

Julia Roberts is a **1)** .... **FAME** actress. She has starred in many **2)** .... films and her latest film, **SUCCESS** *Notting Hill*, is no exception. She plays a **3)** .... film star who becomes **GLAMOUR** romantically involved with an ordinary bookshop owner, played by Hugh Grant. She is trying to take a **4)** .... **PEACE** break from her **5)** .... fans **NUMBER** and ends up staying in Grant's flat along with his **6)** .... flatmate. The **MESS** script is very **7)** .... and **FUN** the film has become very popular. It is a **8)** .... film not to be missed. **WONDER**

Relative Pronouns

- Relative pronouns, **(who(m)**, **which**, **that**, **whose)**, introduce relative clauses. A relative clause gives us information about which particular person or thing the speaker is referring to.
  The girl who works in the bakery is my cousin.

  relative clause

  (The relative clause tells us which girl we are talking about.)
- We use **who/that** to refer to **people**.
  The lady who lives next door has lots of pets.
- We use **which/that** to refer to **things/objects** or **animals**.
  I saw a film which was extremely interesting.
- **Who/Which/That** cannot be omitted when it is the subject of the relative clause.
  She is the girl who lives in the High Street.   *I am reading a book which is very boring.*

  subject   subject

- **Who/Which/That** can be omitted when it is the object of the relative clause, i.e. when there is a noun or personal pronoun between the relative pronoun and the verb.
  I spoke to a woman (who(m)/that) I had met before.   *This is the car (which/that) he bought last week.*

  object   object

- We use **whose** instead of possessive adjectives (*my, your, his, etc.*) with people, objects and animals to show possession.
  This is Mrs Thomas, whose daughter is a doctor.
- A relative pronoun is not used with another pronoun (I, you, me, him, etc.).
  I know the man who ~~he~~ won first prize in the competition.

  Note: • **who's: who is** or **who has**
             ***Who's** she? (= who is)*
             *That's the lady **who's** got an Alsatian dog. (= who has)*
         • **whose: possessive**
             *He's the man **whose** dog bit me.*

Relative Adverbs

Where, **when**, and **why** are relative adverbs and can introduce relative clauses.
- **Where** is used to refer to **place** usually after nouns like *house, hotel, street, town, country*, etc. It can be replaced by **which/that + preposition**. In this case, **which/that** can be omitted.
  *The hotel **where** we stayed was fantastic.*
  *The hotel (which/that) we stayed **at** was fantastic.*
- **When** is used to refer to **time**, usually after nouns like *time, period, moment, day, summer*, etc. It can either be omitted or replaced by **that**.
  *I remember the day **(when)** my son was born.*
  *I remember the day **that** my son was born.*
- **Why** is used to give **reason**, usually after the word *reason*. It can either be omitted or replaced by **that**.
  *The reason **(why)** I can't come to your party is that I'm extremely tired.*
  *The reason **that** I can't come to your party is that I'm extremely tired.*

Position of Prepositions in Relative Clauses

Prepositions can come either before relative pronouns or at the end of the relative clause. However, we usually avoid using them before relative pronouns.
*The company **for which** she works sells computers. (formal use)*
*The company **which** she works **for** sells computers. (informal - usual structure)*
*The company she works **for** sells computers. (everyday English)*

Note: **Who** and **that** are not used after prepositions.
This is the girl with whom I played tennis. (formal)
This is the girl (who) I played tennis with. (informal)

Adverbs of Frequency

- **Adverbs of frequency** (*always, usually, often, sometimes, rarely, seldom, hardly ever, never,* etc.) tell us how often something happens. Adverbs of frequency answer the question **How often ...?**
  *"**How often** do you watch quiz shows?" "I **sometimes** watch quiz shows in the evening."*
- Adverbs of frequency usually come **before** the **main verb** but **after** the verb **to be** and **auxiliary** or **modal verbs** such as *do, can, must,* etc.
- The adverbs **rarely**, **seldom**, and **never** have a negative meaning and **are never used** with the word **not**.
  *Sam **never goes** cycling during the week. Not: Sam ~~never doesn't go~~ cycling during the week.*
- Adverbs of frequency always go **before** the **auxiliary verb** in **short answers**.
  A: Do you listen to the radio?
  *B: Yes, I **sometimes do.***

Relative Pronouns

1 Fill in the gaps using *who, which* or *whose* where necessary, as in the example.

1 Can you tell me *who* took the newspapers from the table?
2 The woman ......who........... made the cake is 80 years old.
3 That is the girl ....who............... has just sold her bike to me.
4 What do you think of the new teacher ...who........ started this year?
5 John's the man ....who............ car broke down last week.
6 Have you got any money ......which.... you can lend me?
7 She's the woman ...whose.... brother is a soldier.
8 I lost the necklace ......which............... my grandmother bought me for my birthday.
9 When are you going to move those boxes ......which.... are in the hall?
10 The man ....who.... owns that shop is retiring next year.

2 Join the sentences using *who* or *which,* as in the example.

1 Nepal is a country. It is situated in Asia.
   *Nepal is a country **which** is situated in Asia.*
2 The Vikings were warriors. They lived in Scandinavia.
   ....who..............
3 Elephants are mammals. They can eat about 225 kilos of grass in one day. which
   ....
4 Alfred Hitchcock was a film director. He made a lot of successful films. who
   ....
5 Clare is an accountant. She works for my father.
   ....who..............
6 A bee is an insect. It makes honey.
   ....which............
7 Carl Lewis is an athlete. He has won several gold medals. who
   ....
8 I watched a documentary. It was extremely interesting. which
   ....

3 Complete each definition using *who* or *which* and the following prompts, as in the example.

- *fix/our teeth*
- *we/eat/in the summer*
- *work/in space*
- *live/in the sea*
- *cut/people's hair*

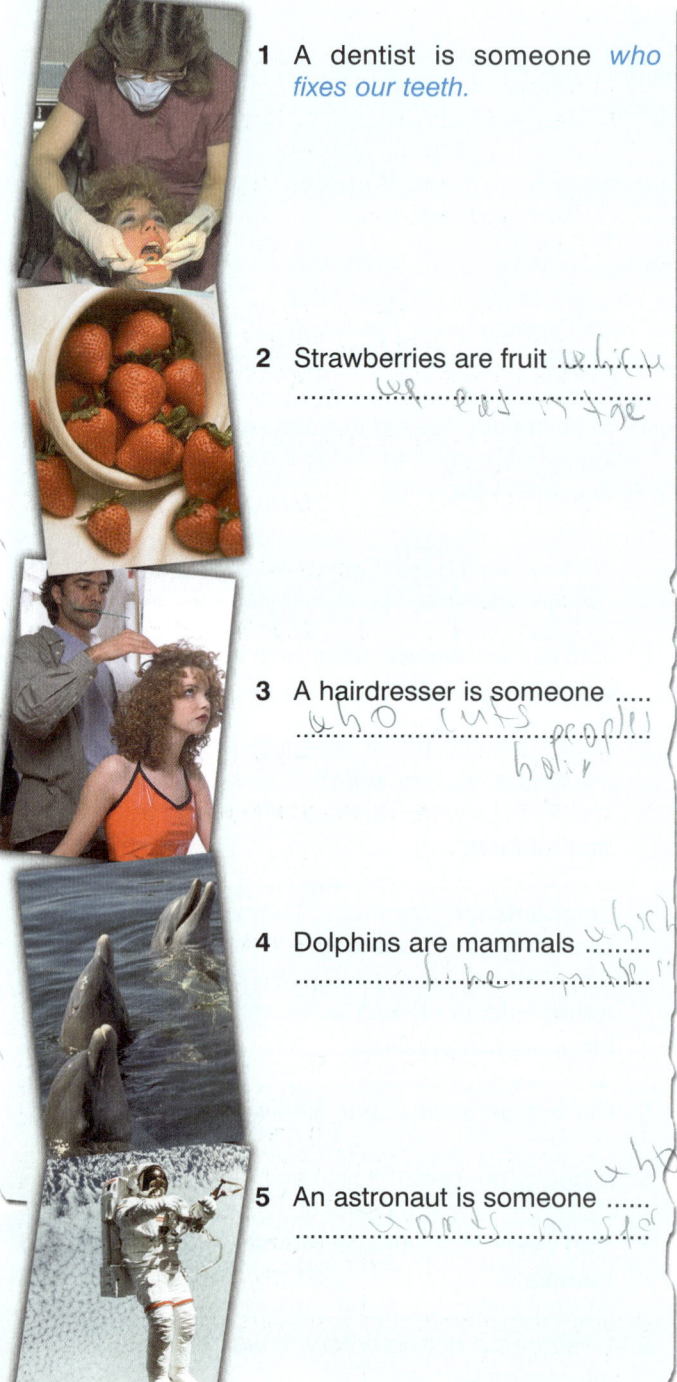

1 A dentist is someone *who fixes our teeth.*

2 Strawberries are fruit .w.h.i.c.h. .... we eat in the summer

3 A hairdresser is someone ..... who cuts people's hair

4 Dolphins are mammals .... which .... like public

5 An astronaut is someone ...... who .... works in spa

4 Join the sentences using *who*, *which* or *whose*, as in the example.

1 Bob is a photographer. His studio is located in the city centre.
*Bob is a photographer **whose** studio is located in the city centre.*

2 Anne works for a large firm. The firm produces cosmetics.   which
....

3 Pamela is an animal lover. She fights for animal rights.   who
....

4 Aristotle was an ancient Greek philosopher. His books are still widely read.   which
....

5 National Geographic is a magazine. It sells millions of copies all over the world.   which
....

6 Frank Sinatra was a famous singer. He sang many beautiful songs.   who
....

7 I live in a village. It is very peaceful and quiet.   where   which
....

8 That is the man. His son is a professional basketball player.   whose
....

5 Underline the correct word.

1 She's the girl **who's**/**whose** got red hair.
2 That's the man **who's**/**whose** car was stolen.
3 That's the boy **who's**/**whose** mother is French.
4 That's the girl **who's**/**whose** name is Marie.
5 He's the man **who's**/**whose** famous for climbing mountains.
6 That's the woman **who's**/**whose** got a garden full of exotic plants.

6 Choose the correct item.

1 The man .... lives down the road is very rich.
A whom   B who   C which

2 .... car is parked in front of our house?
A Whose   B Which   C Who's

3 .... were you talking to on the phone?
A Whom   B Which   C Whose

4 I saw a beautiful carpet .... I want to buy.
A who   B which   C whose

5 Have you finished with the book .... I lent you?
A who   B who's   C that

6 That's the woman .... a school teacher.
A who's　　　　B whose　　　　C who

7 The boy .... sits next to me at school has got three sisters.
A who's　　　　B that　　　　C whose

8 She's the girl .... is going to marry John.
A who　　　　B which　　　　C who's

9 Where are the eggs .... I bought earlier?
A who　　　　B whose　　　　C which

10 This is the shop .... was burgled last night.
A whom　　　　B which　　　　C who's

7 First match the words in the list to the pictures and then use the prompts to make sentences with *who* or *which*, as in the example.

hanger, artist, key, postman, washing machine, mechanic

A **B**

1 hang/clothes on
A hanger is something which you hang clothes on.

2 fix/people's cars
....
....
....

C **D**

3 open and lock/doors with
....
....
....

4 deliver/the post
....
....
....

E **F**

5 wash/clothes in
....
....
....

6 paint/pictures
....
....
....

8 Fill in the gaps with *who*, *which* or *whose*, then choose the correct item to answer the questions.

1 What is the name of the ship .... which sank on its first voyage?
A Titania　　　　B Titanic

2 What is the name of the longest river .... which runs through South America?
A The Amazon　　　　B The Nile

3 What is the name of the actress .... who was very famous in the 1950's?
A Marilyn Monroe　　　　B Sharon Stone

4 What is the name of the country in .... which the Pyramids are situated?
A Egypt　　　　B Morocco

5 What is the name of the actress .... whose husband is Antonio Banderas?
A Melanie Griffith　　　　B Cameron Diaz

6 What is the name of the man .... who invented the telephone?
A Albert Einstein　　　　B Alexander Graham Bell

7 What is the name of the person .... who wrote *Romeo and Juliet*?
A Jules Verne　　　　B William Shakespeare

8 What is the name of the city in .... which the Taj Mahal is located?
A Agra　　　　B Atlanta

9 Link Column A with Column B using the correct relative pronoun.

A	B
1 A lawnmower is a machine	**a** lives in Hollywood.
2 Peter's brother is an actor	**b** you sit on.
3 A flight attendant is a person	**c** father donated lots of money to charity.
4 This is Jane	**d** serves passengers on a plane.
5 A sofa is a piece of furniture	**e** cuts grass.

who whose which

13

Relative Adverbs

10 **Fill in the gaps with *where*, *when* or *why*, as in the example.**

1 This is the neighbourhood ...*where*... I spent most of my childhood.
2 The reason .... Jill can't come to your party is that she has to study for her exams.
3 I remember the day .... Manchester United won the European Cup Final.
4 The little corner shop .... I used to buy my groceries is now a huge supermarket.
5 What's the reason .... Joe didn't come to school today?
6 Tracy didn't realise that the restaurant .... we ate last night was your father's.
7 Rachel didn't explain .... she didn't attend the meeting.
8 Do you remember the time .... we got lost up in the mountains?

11 **Fill in the gaps with *where*, *when* or *why*.**

Dear Andrew,

How are you? The reason **1)** .... I'm writing is to tell you some great news.

Remember **2)** .... you were here last year and we went to that theatre **3)** .... I ran into Sally, an old school friend of mine? Well, guess what? We got married last month! We were in Paris on holiday **4)** .... we got married and that's **5)** .... we didn't invite anyone. We've decided to live in the town **6)** .... we both grew up and we're looking forward to the day **7)** .... we can buy our own house. Anyway, we hope you can come and visit us **8)** .... you have time.

Write back soon and tell me your news.

Love,
Peter

Position of Prepositions in Relative Clauses

12 **Rewrite the sentences in as many ways as possible, as in the example.**

1 That's the house in which I grew up.
That's the house which I grew up in.
That's the house I grew up in.
That's the house where I grew up.
2 That's the island on which they discovered an ancient city.
....
....
3 That's the woman for whom I worked.
....
....
4 That's the boat in which we sailed around the world.
....
....
5 That's the film in which Goldie Hawn stars.
....
....
6 That's the boy with whom I had a fight.
....
....
7 This is the house in which my grandmother was born.
....
....
8 Mrs Cross is the woman for whom I babysit.
....
....

Adverbs of Frequency

13 **Put the *adverbs of frequency* in the correct position, as in the example.**

1 We go out on Saturday evenings. **(always)**
We always go out on Saturday evenings.
2 The children eat junk food. **(hardly ever)**
....
3 They have been abroad. **(never)**
....
4 Do David and Sarah do their homework before dinner? **(always)**
....
5 I see my sister because she lives so far away. **(rarely)**
....
6 Emily cooks dinner for herself. **(seldom)**
....

7 Does Tom do the housework on Tuesday? **(usually)**

....

8 I watch comedy films. **(sometimes)**

....

Revision: Units 1 - 2

Multiple Choice

14 **Choose the correct item.**

1 Lily is a very caring person .... she can be a bit lazy at times.
   A but   **B** and   **C** also

2 I .... my grandparents tomorrow.
   A seeing   **B** 'm seeing   **C** see

3 That is the motorcycle .... Larry bought last month.
   A which   **B** who   **C** whose

4 A: Do you play golf at the weekends?
   B: Yes, I .... do.
   A seldom   **B** never   **C** often

5 John's parents .... on a farm.
   A lives   **B** live   **C** living

6 The restaurant .... we ate last night was amazing.
   A when   **B** where   **C** why

7 Caroline .... the dog at the moment.
   A is walking   **B** walk   **C** walks

8 This is Mr Kane .... wife is a deep-sea diver.
   A which   **B** who's   **C** whose

9 I hate snakes .... I like lizards.
   A but   **B** as well as   **C** and

10 I .... of moving to the country.
   A thinks   **B** am thinking   **C** think

Error Correction

15 **Cross out the unnecessary word.**

1 Is he the man who he has got a white Porsche?
2 This is the restaurant where we ate there last Sunday.
3 This is the shop whose its alarm went off last night.
4 The flat where we stayed at was very small.
5 We rarely not go to the cinema.
6 "Do you like my new hat?" "Yes, I do like."

Key Word Transformation

16 **Complete each sentence with two to five words, including the word in bold.**

1 The animals in the zoo are all endangered species.
   which The animals ....
   .... zoo are all endangered species.

2 That is the hospital I had my operation at.
   where That is the hospital ....
   .... my operation.

3 The restaurant she works in specialises in Italian cuisine.
   which The restaurant ....
   .... specialises in Italian cuisine.

4 Adam is the man; his house was burgled.
   whose Adam is .... burgled.

5 I met a man. He owns a successful business.
   who I met a man ....
   .... successful business.

Word Formation

We can also form adjectives from nouns by adding **-ing**, **-ed** or **-less** e.g. *interest - interesting, talent - talented, care - careless*

17 **Fill in the gaps with the correct words derived from the words in bold.**

Tom Hanks is a very **1)** .... **FAME** actor and has starred in many popular films, including *Sleepless in Seattle* and *Philadelphia*.

Although he is in his early forties, his **2)** .... good looks make **YOUTH** him appear younger than he is.

Tom Hanks is a **3)** .... **CHARM** person who likes being around people. He is also **4)** .... and is **CARE** not afraid to show his feelings for those who are close to him. His love for his family is apparent when he talks about them.

In his free time, Tom Hanks enjoys doing many **5)** .... things. **INTEREST** He is quite a **6)** .... person **REST** who likes to be busy all the time. For example, he loves writing scripts as well as directing films.

He has many fans who admire him a lot because he is a **7)** .... **TALENT** man who hasn't let success change him.

Past Simple: regular verbs

Affirmative	Negative
I walk**ed** You walked He walked She walked It walked We walked You walked They walked	I **didn't** walk You didn't walk, etc.
	Interrogative
	Did I walk? Did you walk?, etc.

Short answers

Did I/you/we, etc. walk ...?	**Yes, I/you/we, etc. did.** **No, I/you/we, etc. didn't.**

Form

- We form the affirmative of most regular verbs by adding **-ed** to the verb.
  *I return - I return**ed***
- Some verbs have irregular affirmative forms.
  *I go - I **went***
  (See list of irregular verbs at the back of the book.)

Spelling

Study these examples:

*I dance - I danc**ed***   *I drop - I drop**ped***
*I try - I tr**ied***   *I cancel - I cancel**led***
*I play - I play**ed***

Use

We use **the past simple** for:
- actions which happened or finished at a definite or stated time in the past.
  *We **left** the house at 7.30 pm.*
- actions which happened repeatedly in the past but do not happen any more. In this case, we can use adverbs of frequency (always, often, usually, etc.).
  *He often **watched** football matches with his brother when he **was** a teenager (but he doesn't any more).*
- actions which happened immediately one after the other in the past.
  *First, he **opened** the window. Then, he **looked** down the street and **saw** a strange black car.*

Time Expressions we use with the past simple:

> yesterday, last night/week/year/Monday, etc., **a month/two years/three years**, etc., **ago, in 1960**, etc.
> *Princess Diana **died in 1997**.*

Past Continuous

Affirmative	Negative
I **was** walk**ing** You **were** walking He was walking She was walking It was walking We were walking You were walking They were walking	I wasn't walking You weren't walking He wasn't walking, etc.
	Interrogative
	Was I walking? Were you walking? Was he walking? etc.

Short answers

Was I/he/she/it walking ...?	**Yes, I/he/she/it was.** **No, I/he/she/it wasn't.**
Were we/you/they walking ...?	**Yes, we/you/they were.** **No, we/you/they weren't.**

Use

We use **the past continuous**:
- for an action which was in progress at a stated time in the past. We do not know when the action started or finished.
  *At 9 o'clock last night we **were watching** TV.*
- for a past action which was in progress when another action interrupted it. We use the **past continuous** for the action in progress (longer action) and the **past simple** for the action which interrupted it (shorter action).
  *She **was cooking** dinner when the doorbell **rang**.*
- for two or more actions which were happening at the same time in the past (simultaneous actions).
  *David **was reading** the newspaper while Carla **was watching** TV.*
- to give background information in a story and to set the scene.
  *The snow **was falling** heavily as Mary **was walking** in the park.*

Time Expressions we use with the past continuous:

> **when, while, as, all day/night/morning**, etc.,
> Note: when/while/as + past continuous (longer action) when + past simple (shorter action)

Present Perfect Simple

Affirmative	Negative
I **have** walk**ed**	I haven't walked
You have walked	You haven't walked
He **has** walk**ed**	He hasn't walked, etc.
She has walked	**Interrogative**
It has walked	
We have walked	Have I walked?
You have walked	Have you walked?
They have walked	Has he walked? etc.

Short answers

Have I/you/we/they walked ...?	Yes, I/you/we/they have. No, I/you/we/they haven't.
Has he/she/it walked ...?	Yes, he/she/it has. No, he/she/it hasn't.

Form

- We form the present perfect simple with **have/has** and the **past participle** of the main verb.
  *John **has broken** the vase in the living room.*
- We form the past participle of regular verbs by adding **-ed** to the verb.
  *clean - clean**ed***
- We form the past participle of irregular verbs differently. *buy - bought, write - written* (See list of irregular verbs at the back of the book.)

Use

We use **the present perfect simple** for:
- a recent action which happened at an unstated time in the past.
  *Debbie **has just moved** into a new house.*
- an action which started in the past and is still continuing in the present.
  *They **have been** teachers since 1987.*
- an action which has recently finished and whose results are visible in the present.
  *The chocolate cake he **has made** is on the table.*

- personal experiences or changes.
  *Bob **has put on** weight.*

Have gone (to) - Have been (to)

The verb **go** has got two present perfect forms: **have gone** and **have been**.

Study the examples to see the difference in meaning.

***She has gone to** Austria. (She is still in Austria; she hasn't come back yet.)*
***She has been to** Austria twice this year. (She has visited Austria, but she has returned.)*

Time Expressions we use with the present perfect simple:

> **since, for, just, already, yet, lately, recently, so far, ever, never**, etc.
> - *So far she has baked three cakes.*
> - *Have you **ever** been to Madrid?*
> - *We have **never** seen a blue whale.*

since (= from a starting point in the past)
*since 1990, **since** last Friday, etc.*

for (= over a period of time)
*for two years, **for** nine months, etc.*

Just and **already** are used in affirmative sentences.
*He has **already** washed the car.*
*They have **just** arrived.*

Yet is used in questions and negations.
*Have you called a taxi **yet**?*
*She hasn't finished **yet**.*

Present Perfect Continuous

Affirmative	Negative
I**'ve been** walk**ing**	I haven't been walking
You've been walking	You haven't been walking
He**'s been** walking	He hasn't been walking, etc.
She's been walking	**Interrogative**
It's been walking	
We've been walking	Have I been walking?
You've been walking	Have you been walking?
They've been walking	Has he been walking? etc.

Use

We use **the present perfect continuous**
- to put emphasis on the duration of an action which started in the past and continues in the present.
  *They **have been working** in the garden for two hours.*
- for an action which started in the past and lasted for some time. The action may have finished or may still be going on. The result of the action is visible in the present.
  *Mary has a stomach ache. She **has been eating** chocolate all morning.*

Short answers

Have I/you/we/they been walking ...?	Yes, I/you/we/they have. No, I/you/we/they haven't.
Has he/she/it been walking ...?	Yes, he/she/it has. No, he/she/it hasn't.

Time Expressions we use with the present perfect continuous:

for, since, lately, all morning/week, etc.
- *He hasn't been feeling well **lately**.*
- *I have been cleaning the house **all morning**.*

Past Simple - Past Continuous

1 **Put the verbs in brackets into the correct form of the past simple. Which use of the past simple does each sentence show?**

1 Michael .... (watch) a great film last night.
2 Tom .... (come) home late, ... (eat) a sandwich and .... (go) to bed.
3 I always .... (enjoy) reading fairy tales when I was young.
4 Mrs Smith .... (arrive) at the office, ... (turn on) the computer and .... (start) typing.
5 .... (you/study) hard when you were at university?
6 My father .... (not/fight) in the Second World War.
7 Forty years ago, my grandmother .... (walk) two kilometres to school every day.
8 Last year, Tom .... (give) his wife a new car for her birthday.

2 **Put the verbs in brackets into the correct form of the past simple, as in the example.**

1 A: What **1)** ...*did you do*... (you/do) last weekend?
  B: I **2)** .... (spend) the weekend camping in the mountains.
  A: Really! **3)** .... (be) the weather nice?
  B: No, it **4)** .... (rain) every day.

2 A: Where did Sally go yesterday afternoon?
  B: She **1)** .... (go) to hospital.
  A: Why?
  B: She **2)** .... (slip) on a banana skin and **3)** .... (break) her leg.
3 A: **1)** .... (Bob and Sue/be) at Jeff's party last night?
  B: No, I **2)** .... (not/see) them, but Jim **3)** .... (tell) me later that they **4)** .... (be) on holiday.

3 **A policeman is asking a witness about an accident he saw. Put the verbs in brackets into the past simple or the past continuous, as in the example.**

P: Where **1)** ...*were*... (be) you when you **2)** .... (see) the accident, Sir?
W: I **3)** .... (stand) on the corner of Jameson Street.
P: What exactly **4)** .... (happen)?
W: Well, a boy **5)** .... (ride) his bicycle along the road towards the traffic lights when suddenly a car **6)** .... (drive) quickly around the corner. The driver **7)** .... (lose) control and **8)** .... (hit) the boy.
P: **9)** .... (boy/cycle) fast?
W: No, not at all.
P: **10)** .... (anyone else/see) the accident?
W: No, I don't think so.
P: Thank you very much for your help, Sir.

4 *The fire alarm went off at the Royal Hotel last night.* Look at the picture and put the verbs in the list into the past continuous to describe what each person was doing, as in the example.

pay, read, carry, talk

1 When the fire alarm went off Mrs Brown ...*was reading* ... a book.
2 A man .....*was talking*....... on the phone.
3 Two men .....*were paying*.......... their bill.
4 A porter .....*was carrying*........... some suitcases.

5 Underline the correct form of the verb.

1 He *slept*/*was sleeping* at 10 o'clock this morning.
2 We all *went*/*were going* out last night.
3 I *ate*/*was eating* breakfast when the phone *rang*/*was ringing*.
4 I *took*/*was taking* some really great photos when I *was*/*was being* in California.
5 She *had*/*was having* lunch with her fiancé when he *gave*/*was giving* her an expensive ring as a birthday present.
6 He *met*/*was meeting* Mary yesterday.

Present Perfect Simple

6 Put the verbs in brackets into the present perfect simple.

1 A: Why don't you stay at home and finish your homework?
   B: I ...*have already finished*... (already/finish) it.
2 A: How long ...*have they known*....... (they/know) each other?
   B: For more than ten years.

3 A: ...*Have you seen*......... (you/see) Carl lately?
   B: No, I ...*haven't seen*......... (not/see) him since Christmas.
4 A: ...*Has Mike ridden*......... (Mike/ride) a motorcycle before?
   B: No, he hasn't.
5 A: Mum ...*has already cooked*......... (already/cook) dinner, hasn't she?
   B: No, she ...*hasn't started*......... (not/start) cooking it yet.
6 A: Can I have a piece of cake?
   B: Sorry, Sue ...*has just had*........... (just/have) the last piece.

Have gone (to) - Have been (to)

7 Fill in the gaps with *have*/*has gone* or *have*/*has been*.

1 Mum ...*has gone*......... to the supermarket. She'll be home soon.
2 ...*Have*... you ever ...*been*... to the opera?
3 My sister ...*has gone*......... to the cinema. She left an hour ago.
4 We ...*have been*........... to Paris twice so far this year but we want to go again soon.
5 My brother ...*has*... never ...*been*....... to an art gallery.
6 He ...*has gone*......... to school. He should be home by 4.00.
7 Peter ...*has*...... just ...*gone*......... to the corner shop. He'll be back in a minute.
8 James ...*has gone*......... to Manchester for a few days on a business trip. He's returning tomorrow.

Present Perfect Continuous

8 Fill in the gaps with the present perfect continuous form of the verbs in the list below, as in the example.

talk, wait, work, ride

1 She's bored. Her mum ...*has been talking*... on the phone for an hour.

2 He's happy. He *has been riding* his new bike all day.

3 She is tired. She *has been waiting* since 7.00 this morning.

4 He's worried. He *has been waiting* for an important phone call for an hour.

9 Underline the correct word(s).

1 A: Is Bill still having lunch?
B: No, he has **just**/yet finished.
2 Mum was cooking dinner since/**while** Dad was washing the car.
3 We first met almost thirty years **ago**/for.
4 I'm so tired. I haven't slept properly so far/**for** a week.
5 We have **already**/ever been to Australia so we are going to Africa this summer.
6 Jane's **never**/lately been skiing before.
7 Ed has lived in Poland when/**since** 1992.
8 We've been very lucky that it hasn't snowed while/**yet** this winter.
9 That's the most beautiful necklace I've **ever**/yet seen.
10 A: Have you seen Debbie ago/**lately**?
B: No, she has gone to Brazil.

Past Simple - Past Continuous - Present Perfect Simple - Present Perfect Continuous

10 Put the verbs in brackets into the past simple, past continuous, present perfect simple or present perfect continuous.

1 A: Why is Carol tired?
B: She ..... *has been cleaning* ..... **(clean)** the house all morning.
2 "..... *Have you seen* ..... **(you/see)** my watch? I ..... *have been looking* ..... **(look for)** it since yesterday."
3 A: ..... *Did you have* ..... **(you/have)** a good time last night?
B: Yes, the party ..... *was* ..... **(be)** great.
4 A: ..... *Have you been cooking* ..... **(you/cook)** all morning?
B: No, I ..... *have just started* ..... **(just/start)**.
5 A: Where ..... *have you been* ..... **(you/be)**? I ..... *have been calling* ..... **(call)** you all afternoon.
B: I ..... *was working* ..... **(work)** in the basement and I ..... *did not hear* ..... **(not/hear)** the phone.
6 A: What ..... *were you doing* ..... **(you/do)** when the storm ..... *began* ..... **(begin)**?
B: I ..... *was driving* ..... **(drive)** to work.
7 A: Where's Dad?
B: He is in the garage. He ..... *has been repairing* ..... **(repair)** the car all morning.
8 A: ..... *Have you finished* ..... **(you/finish)** packing your suitcase yet?
B: Almost. How about you?

Revision: Units 1 - 3

Multiple Choice

11 Choose the correct item.

1 Cindy .... the party at midnight.
A was leaving   B has left   **C left**
2 The car .... has a flat tyre is mine.
A whose   **B which**   C who
3 Donna .... working very hard lately.
A has been   B was   C have been
4 The reason .... I can't buy a new bicycle is that I haven't got any money.
A why   B which   C for

20

3

5 The boys were playing basketball while their father .... the lawn.
A was mowing   **B** has mowed   **C** mows

6 Lesley is an energetic person. ...., she can be a bit arrogant at times.
A Also   **B** As well   **C** However

7 A: Do you read newspapers?
B: No, I .... do.
A usually   **B** often   **C** never

8 This is the village .... I grew up.
A which   **B** where   **C** what

9 He's been living in the same flat ..... twenty years.
A just   **B** for   **C** since

10 I .... Rachel for dinner later tonight.
A am seeing   **B** saw   **C** have seen

Error Correction

12 Cross out the unnecessary word.

1 This is Alison whose son he is studying at Oxford University.
2 Have they been taken the dog for a walk?
3 The Cooks are being looking for a new house at the moment.
4 The man for whom that he works is German.
5 The play has started an hour ago.
6 When was the last time you have visited your parents?
7 Has Angie left for the airport since?
8 I haven't talked to him since he has left school.

Key Word Transformation

13 Study the table, then complete each sentence with two to five words, including the word in bold.

- They started cleaning an hour ago.
  have   They **have been cleaning** for an hour.
- How long is it since you went abroad?
  ago   How long **ago did you go** abroad?
- She hasn't called yet.
  still   She **still hasn't** called.
- He has never flown in a helicopter before.
  time   It's the **first time he has flown** in a helicopter.
- It's a long time since he worked overtime.
  for   He **hasn't worked overtime for** a long time.

1 He hasn't fixed the washing machine yet.
still   He is still high fixed the washing machine.
2 It's a long time since the band toured Europe.
for   The band hasn't toured to a long time.
3 John started cooking two hours ago.
has   John has been cooking for two hours.
4 She has never been to Paris before.
first   It's the first time in her been to Paris.
5 How long ago did you meet her?
since   How long is it since you met her?

Word Formation

> We use the following suffixes to form adjectives from verbs.
>
> **-able**   e.g. love - love**able**
> **-ive**   e.g. impress - impress**ive**

14 Fill in the gaps with the correct words derived from the words in bold.

Dear Philip,

I am just writing to tell you what a
1) .... holiday we had. We went on   **MARVEL**
a camping holiday to the South of France
and the weather was **2)** wonderful.   **WONDER**
The tent we stayed in was very
3) comfortable . It had a   **COMFORT**
cooker, a fridge and a TV. We were in the
heart of the French countryside and
some of the views were great. The
campsite itself was **4)** impressive.   **IMPRESS**
It was well **5)** organised and the   **ORGANISE**
staff were very **6)** helpful .   **HELP**

There was lots to do and, although I'm
not a very **7)** active person, I   **ACT**
enjoyed swimming and playing tennis. All
in all, it was a very **8)** enjoyable   **ENJOY**
holiday. You should go if you get the
chance. I can send you the brochure if you
like.

Love from
Linda

The Definite Article 'The'

- The definite article **the** is used with both countable and uncountable nouns.
  ***the** egg* (c), ***the** air* (u)

Pronunciation

The is pronounced:
- /ðɪ/ before words which begin with a vowel sound: ***the** office*
- /ðə/ before words which begin with a consonant sound: ***the** N*ile

Use

We use **the:**

- **to talk about something specific, that is, something we have mentioned before or which is already known.**
  *Joe bought a house on King Street. **The** house is very big and **the** street is quiet. (Which house? **The one Joe bought**. Which street? **King Street**.)*
- **with nouns which are unique** (**the** sun, **the** moon)
- **with the names of rivers** (**the** Amazon), **seas** (**the** Mediterranean), **oceans** (**the** Atlantic), **mountain ranges** (**the** Andes), **deserts** (**the** Sahara), **groups of islands** (**the** Virgin Islands) **and countries when they include words such as state, kingdom, republic, etc.** (**the** United Kingdom).
- **with the names of musical instruments** (**the** guitar) **and dances** (**the** waltz), **etc.**
- **with the names of museums** (**the** National Museum), **hotels** (**the** Hilton), **theatres/cinemas** (**the** Royal Theatre), **newspapers** (**The** Guardian), **etc.**
- **with nationalities** (**the** French) **and names of families** (**the** Browns), **etc.**
- **with historical periods/events** (**the** Iron Age, **the** Second World War **but:** World War II), **etc.**
- **with the words** *morning, afternoon, station, city, village,* **etc.**
  *He gets up at 6 o'clock in **the morning**.*
  *They drove into **the city**.*
- **with adjectives used as nouns to refer to a group of people e.g. the poor, the blind, the sick, etc.**
  *She always helps **the poor**.*
- **with only, last, first used as adjectives and with the superlative degree of adjectives/adverbs.**
  *He was **the first** person to leave.*
  *She is **the most intelligent** person I know.*

- **with titles when the name of the person is not mentioned** (**the** President, **the** Prince **but:** Prince Charles).

We do **not** use **the** with:

- **uncountable and plural countable nouns when we talk about something in general.**
  ***Koalas** live in Australia.*
- **proper nouns** *This is **Anna**.*
- **names of countries** (*Brazil*) (**but:** *The Netherlands*), **cities** (*Glasgow*), **streets** (*Oxford Street* **but:** *The High Street*), **parks** (*Hyde Park*), **bridges** (*London Bridge*), **continents** (*Europe*), **squares** (*Leicester Square*), **stations** (*Charing Cross Station*), **islands** (*Rhodes*), **lakes** (*Lake Geneva*), **etc.**
- **two-word names when the first is the name of a person or place.** (*Heathrow Airport*)
- **names of meals** (*dinner*), **sports/games** (*tennis, chess*), **months** (*July*), **celebrations** (*Mardi Gras*), **colours** (*red*), **drinks** (*coffee*) **and languages when they are not followed by the word language.**
  *I speak **Portuguese**. but: **The Portuguese language** is spoken in Brazil.*
- **the words** *school, college, church, bed, court, hospital, prison, university, home,* **etc. when we refer to the purpose for which they exist.**
  *Jim's in **hospital**. (as a patient)*
  *We went to **the hospital** to visit Jim.*
- **the words this/that/these/those** (**this** boy, **those** trees) **NOT:** ~~the~~ this boy
- **possessive adjectives or the possessive case**
  *That isn't **my** house - it's Sue's.*
- **means of transport** (**by bus/train**, etc.)
  *Are you travelling to Paris **by train**?*

Clauses of Result: So/Such (a/an)

Clauses of result are used to express the result of something. They are introduced with:

so/such (a) ... (that), etc.

We use **so:**

- **with adjectives and adverbs.**
  *The restaurant is **so popular (that)** you have to book a table a week in advance.*
  *It was snowing **so heavily (that)** I couldn't see where I was going.*
- **with much/little + uncountable nouns and many/few + countable nouns in the plural.**
  *There was **so much noise (that)** I couldn't study.*

There was **so little space** for my car **(that)** I couldn't park it.
There were **so many books** to read **(that)** I didn't know where to start.
There were **so few hotels** in the village **(that)** we had to go somewhere else.

- **before an adjective which is not followed by a noun.**
  The car was **so expensive (that)** I decided not to buy it.

We use **such** before:

- **a(n) + adjective + singular countable noun**.
  It was **such a funny story (that)** everyone laughed.
- **adjective + plural noun/uncountable noun**.
  It was **such bad news (that)** she started crying.
- **a lot of + plural noun/uncountable noun**.
  There was **such a lot of snow (that)** we couldn't get out of the house.

The Definite Article *The*

1 Fill in *the* where necessary.

1 .... Ganges is a river which runs through India.
2 I would love to meet .... John in person.
3 She went to France by .... train.
4 Jack's mother is in .... France on holiday.
5 Could you show me the way to .... Victoria Park, please?
6 I can meet you outside .... Hilton Hotel tonight at nine o'clock.
7 Where is .... Kalahari Desert?
8 .... leopards live in the jungle.
9 He is reading a book about .... World War I.
10 Have you ever seen .... Great Wall of China?
11 Let's meet in .... Macey's Restaurant.
12 He buys .... *Observer* every morning.
13 They drove to .... north of .... England.
14 Can you please tell me .... way to .... nearest hospital?
15 Did you visit .... Acropolis when you were in .... Athens?
16 People from .... United Kingdom are not .... only people who speak .... English language.
17 A: Where are .... boys?
   B: They're playing .... football on .... beach.
18 I never drive to .... office. I always go on .... foot.
19 Which city in .... England is .... Tower Bridge located in?
20 .... May is my favourite month of .... year.

2 Underline the correct word(s).

1 Chris went diving in **Red Sea/the Red Sea**.
2 **The Taj Mahal/Taj Mahal** is in India.
3 During their trip to New York, John and Mary plan to visit **the Museum of Modern Art/Museum of Modern Art**.
4 Woody Allen is a famous film director who also plays **saxophone/the saxophone**.
5 I have booked a seat on a flight which leaves at 8 o'clock in **the evening/evening**.
6 Geraldine speaks **the Japanese/Japanese** fluently.
7 In a few weeks, **Grays/the Grays** are planning to move to the seaside.
8 She stayed out in **sun/the sun** too long.
9 According to the latest press reports, **the Prime Minister/Prime Minister** is going to resign.
10 They had a guide with them when they climbed **Himalayas/the Himalayas**.
11 I'm extremely tired. The only thing I want is to go to **the bed/bed**.
12 Sam and Pat played **chess/the chess** for hours yesterday afternoon.
13 Life in big cities can be very difficult for **elderly/the elderly**.
14 Did you remember to go to **supermarket/the supermarket** on your way home?
15 Did you pay much for **computer/the computer** you bought?
16 We always eat **dinner/the dinner** at seven o'clock.
17 James is always **first/the first** person to arrive at a party.
18 Let me introduce you to **the Walter/Walter**.
19 My greatest dream is to travel across **the South America/South America**.
20 We spent three weeks at **Hyatt/The Hyatt**. The service was excellent.

3 Fill in *the* where necessary.

1 A: Have you ever been to 1) ....the.... Louvre in Paris?
   B: Yes, but I didn't really like 2) ..the.... glass pyramid!
   A: That's called 3) .... modern art.
   B: Ah, 4) ...the.... Mona Lisa is more my style.

2 A: Did you see 1) ...the.... President on television last week?
   B: Yes. 2) ...the.... speech he made was excellent.
   A: And they say he is going to 3) ...the.... United Kingdom on a visit next month.
   B: Really? That's interesting.

3 A: What a great car!
   B: Thanks. I bought it 1) .... yesterday.
   A: What did you do with 2) ...the.... old one?
   B: I sold it to a friend.

4 A: Have you finished reading 1) ...the.... book I lent you?
   B: I'm on 2) ...the.... last chapter.
   A: What did you think of 3) ...the.... story?
   B: I liked it, but I prefer 4) .... romances.

4 Read the following text and put a tick (✓) for every correct use of *the* and a cross (✗) for every incorrect use of it.

1 The last month was a very exciting month. ...✗...
2 My husband and I went to the Paris ...✗...
3 for our fifth anniversary. The hotel ...✓...
4 we stayed at was located on the south ...✓...
5 bank of the Seine. We had a fantastic view ...✓...
6 of the city from our balcony. We visited ...✓...
7 the Notre Dame and took pictures ...✓...
8 of the Galleries Lafayette. We also tasted ...✓...
9 some delicious the French cuisine and ...✗...
10 danced the night away at one of ...✓...
11 the France's famous nightclubs. ...✗...

So/Such (a/an)

5 Fill in the gaps with *so, such* or *such a(n)*.

1 She runs ....so...... fast that she will surely win the championship.
2 Chris is ...such a..... generous person that he is always giving his friends gifts.
3 The music at the party next door was ...so..... loud that I couldn't sleep.
4 How can you swim in ...such... cold water?
5 We had ....such....... great time when we were in Dublin that we want to go again.
6 There was ...so.....: much noise in the room I found it impossible to concentrate.
7 There were ...so..... few people at the meeting we had to cancel it.
8 She studies ...so..... little that it's amazing she passes her exams.
9 He's ...such... arrogant person that he never admits that he is wrong.
10 Have you ever seen ...such.. polite children before?

6 Complete each sentence with two to five words, including the word in bold.

1 The weather was so hot that we couldn't sleep at night.
   such   It was ...*such hot weather (that)*... we couldn't sleep at night.
2 It was such a lovely holiday resort that we wanted to stay a bit longer.
   so   The holiday resort was ....
   .... to stay a bit longer.
3 The dress was so small that it didn't fit me.
   such   It was ....
   .... that it didn't fit me.
4 It was such a funny film that we couldn't stop laughing.
   so   The film ....
   .... we couldn't stop laughing.
5 That woman is so rich that she can afford to buy herself an aeroplane.
   such   She's ....
   .... she can afford to buy herself an aeroplane.
6 It was such a cold room that we kept our coats on.
   so   The room was ....
   .... our coats on.
7 The house was so old that the Greens decided to look for another one.
   such   It was ....the Greens decided to look for another one.

Revision: Units 1 - 4

Multiple Choice

7 **Choose the correct item.**

1 .... car is that parked in front of the gate?
A Who   **B Whose**   C Where

2 He's .... late for school. He finds it hard to wake up.
A hardly   **B always**   C seldom

3 It's a waste of time trying to talk him out of it. He never .... to anyone.
A listens   B listening   C listened

4 Kevin .... his homework when someone knocked on the door.
A was doing   B does   C did

5 Yesterday, we .... at an excellent Chinese restaurant.
A have dined   B are dining   **C dined**

6 Mary .... to her ballet lesson yesterday because she was ill.
A didn't go   B hasn't gone   C wasn't going

7 He's been doing the same job .... he was twenty years old.
A since   B for   C before

8 I .... the train to Prague tomorrow.
A am catching   B was catching   C caught

9 Bob was trying to open the front door .... the police arrived.
A while   B which   **C when**

10 Ron has already .... the balcony.
A clean   **B cleaned**   C cleaning

Error Correction

8 **Cross out the unnecessary word.**

1 He is travelling to Manchester by ~~the~~ train.
2 I saw the man who ~~he~~ lives upstairs.
3 ~~The~~ Rome is the capital of Italy.
4 While Melanie was studying in her room ~~and~~ she heard a strange noise.
5 It was such ~~a~~ nice weather that we went to the beach.
6 We went to England ~~for~~ two years ago.
7 ~~The~~ May is my favourite month.
8 It was such ~~a~~ good news that she couldn't believe it.

Key Word Transformation

9 **Complete each sentence with two to five words, including the word in bold.**

1 It's the first time Frank has driven a car.
never   Frank *has never driven* .... a car before.

2 John started taking French lessons five years ago.
been   John *has been started taking* .... *French lessons* for five years.

3 How long ago did you live in Venezuela?
since   How long is it *since you* .... *lived* .... in Venezuela?

4 Paula hasn't come home from the cinema yet.
still   Paula *still hasn't come* .... *home* .... from the cinema.

5 It was such a good film that I'm going to see it again tonight.
so   The film *was so good* .... I'm going to see it again tonight.

Word Formation

10 **Fill in the gaps with the correct words derived from the words in bold.**

India is one of the largest and most
1) *wonderful* countries in the world. Apart **WONDER**
from its **2)** *fantastic* cultural and **FANTASY**
linguistic variety, it's also known for its
food which is extremely **3)** *tasty* . Its **TASTE**
most famous dish is curry. There are hot
and **4)** *spicy* curries as well as sweet **SPICE**
and mild ones. With its magnificent
temples, its long **5)** *sandy* beaches **SAND**
and its unique cuisine, India is a truly
6) *delightful* country well worth visiting. **DELIGHT**

Used to

Used to is used to talk about past habits or things that do not happen any more. It has the same form in all persons, singular and plural and it is followed by the infinitive.
Karen **used to eat** a lot of sweets. (She doesn't eat a lot of sweets any more.)
We form questions and negations with the auxiliary verb **did/did not (didn't)**, **the subject** and **the verb "use" without -d**.
*Did Karen **use to eat** a lot of sweets?*
*Karen **didn't use to eat** a lot of sweets.*
To talk about past habits that do not happen any longer we can use the past simple instead of "used to" with no difference in meaning.
*He **used to ride** a motorcycle.*
*ALSO: He **rode** a motorcycle.*

Linking Words

- To introduce actions that happened or were happening in the past when another action was taking place we can use: **when**, **while**, **as**, etc.
*She was typing a letter **when** her boss called her into his office.*
*Tom was listening to the radio **while** his mother was watching TV.*
- To introduce cause/reason or effect/result we can use **as**, **because**, **so**, etc.
*She didn't go to the party **because** she was tired.*
*Katie was practising hard **as** she wanted to do well in the tennis tournament.*
*I was thirsty **so** I drank a glass of water.*

Used to

1 Complete the sentences with the correct form of *used to* and the verbs in brackets, as in the example.

1 Sandra ...*used to live*... **(live)** in Rome, but now she lives in Paris.
2 The Krafts ....*didn't use to*.............. **(not/have)** any pets, but now they have four dogs.
3 Dave ....*used to* ....*wear*....... **(wear)** jeans and T-shirts when he was younger, but now he wears suits.
4 ....*Did* ......*you use to go*............. **(you/go)** to the cinema every week when you were a child?
5 We ....*used to* .... **(eat)** meat, but now we only eat vegetables.
6 George ....*used to be*............. **(be)** lazy when he was a child, but now he's very energetic.

2 Rewrite each person's comments using *used to* or *didn't use to*, as in the examples.

1 Deborah - I don't work in a clothes shop any more.

...*She used to work in a clothes shop*....

2 Don - I've got a motorcycle now.

...*He didn't use to have a motorcycle*.....

3 Janet - I live on a boat now.

She didn't use to
live on a boat
....

4 Adam - I haven't got a beard now.

He used to have a beard
....

5 Lou - I grow my own vegetables now.

He didn't use to grow
....

6 Kate - I don't watch TV every day any more.

She used to watch
....

7 Peter - I go to the theatre once a week now.

He didn't use to
....

8 Anne - I know how to use a computer now.

She didn't use to
....

Linking Words

3 Join the sentences below using *when, while, so* or *as/because*, as in the example.

1 They were having lunch.	**a** It started to snow.
2 Emily was having a bath.	**b** I took a taxi to work.
3 I woke up late.	**c** They were hungry.
4 We were walking in the park.	**d** Peter was making dinner.

1 ...*They were having lunch* **because**/*as they were hungry*....

2 *Emily was having a bath when Peter...*

3 *I woke up late, so I took a taxi...*

4 *...were walking in the park when it started to snow...*

4 Underline the correct word.

1 **When/While** did he arrive?

2 **Because/As** Susan was painting the fence, she tripped over the dog.

3 Harry was tired, **because/so** he went to bed early.

4 What were they doing **when/so** the burglar broke into their house?

5 **While/When** you were reading the paper, I was cooking dinner.

6 Alice couldn't fix the dishwasher by herself, **so/as** she called a repairman.

5 Complete the sentences using *so* or *because*.

1 We overslept ...*because*... the alarm clock didn't go off.

2 I'm really tired ...*because*... I stayed up late last night.

3 The library was closed, ...*so*... we went to the bookshop instead.

4 I was bored ...*because*... I had nothing to do.

5 Jean was hungry, ...*so*... she made herself a sandwich.

Past Simple vs Past Continuous

6 Put the verbs in brackets into the past simple or the past continuous, as in the example. Which is the longer action in each sentence?

1 As we ...*were surfing*... **(surf)** the Internet we ...*found*... **(find)** a website about horoscopes. ...*surfing the Internet is the longer action*...

2 Ed ...*was leaving*... **(leave)** the house when he ...*heard*... **(hear)** the phone ring.

3 They ...*saw*... **(see)** a little boy run into an abandoned building as they ...*were driving*... **(drive)** down the deserted street.

4 It ...*started*... **(start)** to rain as we ...*were waiting*... **(wait)** at the bus stop.

5 Sarah ...*was writing a*... **(write)** a letter when the lights ...*went out*... **(go out)**.

6 My brother ...*was tidying*... **(tidy)** his room when he ...*found*... **(find)** his old toys.

7 Judy ...*was cycling*... **(cycle)** to work when suddenly her bike ...*got*... **(get)** a flat tyre.

7 Look at the pictures, then put the verbs in brackets into the past simple or the past continuous, as in the example.

1 Ted ...*was sleeping*... **(sleep)** when his father ...*left*... **(leave)** for work.

2 As Kelly ...*was leaving*... **(leave)** for the school trip, her mother ...*gave*... **(give)** her a lunch box to take with her.

27

3 They *were practising* .... **(practise)** for their concert when their mother .... *called* ..... **(call)** them to have lunch.

4 They *were writing* **(write)** on the board when the teacher .... *came* **(come)** in.

5 Carol .... *was putting* **(put)** the shopping into the car when David ..... *saw* .... **(see)** her.

6 Marcus ..... *was* .... *working* **(work)** on his laptop when the phone ..... *rang* .... **(ring).**

8 Put the verbs in brackets into the past simple or the past continuous, as in the example.

A When Alison **1)** ...*arrived*... **(arrive)** home she **2)** .... *took off* .... **(take off)** her wet shoes and **3)** .... *hang* .... **(hang)** up her coat. Outside, the wind **4)** ..... *was blowing* . **(blow)** wildly and the windows **5)** ...... *were rattling* .... **(rattle).** She **6)** .... *was walking* ..**(walk)** into the kitchen, **7)** .... *fed* .... **(feed)** the cat and **8)** .... *was* .... **(be)** just about to make herself a sandwich when she **9)** .... *heard* .... **(hear)** someone whisper her name.

B We **1)** ..... *were having* .... **(have)** dinner when the doorbell **2)** .. *rang* .... **(ring).** My father **3)** ..... *got up* .... **(get up)** and **4)** .... *opened* ...... **(open)** the door. A man **5)** .... *came* .... **(come)** rushing in. "I'm sorry to bother you," he said, "but my wife and I **6)** ...... *were driving* .... **(drive)** along the road when we **7)** ..... *had* .... **(have)** an accident. There **8)** .... *was* .... **(be)** no one to help us so I **9)** .... *came* .... **(come)** here."

9 Use the prompts below to ask and answer questions, as in the example.

1 The library caught fire.
   - read book/on first floor
   - run to/emergency exit
   A: ...*What were you doing when the library caught fire?* ...
   B: ...*I was reading a book on the first floor.*...
   A: ...*What did you do?*...
   B: ...*I ran to the emergency exit.*...

2 The car crashed.
   - walk down/street
   - call/police

3 The film star arrived.
   - wait/in the queue
   - ask for/autograph

4 The earthquake hit.
   - sleep/in my bed
   - dive under/the table

Revision: Units 1 - 5

Multiple Choice

10 **Choose the correct item.**

1 That's the woman .... husband is a musician.
   A who   **B** who's   **C** whose

2 .... Alice go to the rock concert on Saturday night?
   A Did   **B** Do   **C** Does

3 Where is .... Amazon Rainforest located?
   A an   **B** the   **C** —

4 It was .... lovely day that we ate in the garden.
   A such   **B** so   **C** such a

5 The shop .... I bought my jacket is in the city centre.
   A when   **B** that   **C** where

6 The sun .... brightly as Steve walked to work.
   A was shining **B** is shining   **C** shine

7 Have you .... been to Thailand?
   A lately   **B** yet   **C** ever

8 Sue is a caring person .... she tends to be a bit rude at times.
   A but   **B** and   **C** also

Error Correction

11 Cross out the unnecessary word.

1 That's the man whose his sister is a singer.
2 Jane she looked out of the window.
3 The sun was shining and the birds were singing too.
4 What is the name of the man who he discovered America?
5 He was hungry so that he made a sandwich.
6 The Nile is in the Egypt.
7 The hotel in where we stayed was fabulous.
8 She doesn't speak the Spanish.

Key Word Transformation

12 Study the table, then complete each sentence with two to five words, including the word in bold.

- It is such a short dress that I can't wear it.
  too   The dress **is too short for me** to wear.
- The last time I saw Mary was two weeks ago.
  seen   I **haven't seen Mary for** two weeks.
- How long is it since you left school?
  leave How **long ago did you leave** school?

1 We haven't had a barbecue for three years.
   had   The last time ....
   .... was three years ago.

2 How long is it since she published her first book?
   ago   How ....
   .... her first book?

3 It was such an expensive watch that I couldn't buy it.
   too   The watch .... to buy.

4 How long ago did she leave for Japan?
   left   How long is it ....
   .... for Japan?

5 The last time I saw Molly was at Bob's birthday party.
   seen   I ....
   .... Bob's birthday party.

6 The house is too small for us to live in.
   such   It is ....
   .... we can't live in it.

Word Formation

We usually form adverbs by adding - **ly** to the adjective.
quick - quickly
Adjectives ending in **consonant + y** drop the -y and take **-ily**. *easy - easily*
Adjectives ending in **-l** take **-ly**.
careful - carefully
Adjectives ending in **-ic** usually take **-ally**.
specific - specifically
Adjectives ending in **-le** drop the -e and take **-y**.
probable - probably
Adjectives ending in **-e** take **-ly**.
polite - politely **But:** *true - truly*

13 Fill in the gaps with the correct words derived from the words in bold.

1 I knew she was asleep as she was breathing ....heavily........... (**heavy**).
2 It is ...widely....... (**wide**) known that smoking can cause cancer.
3 Mr Clark's brother was ...tragically....... (**tragic**) killed in a boating accident last year.
4 The figures can't ...possibly........... (**possible**) be wrong! I checked them myself!
5 The witness answered the lawyer's question ....immediately........(**immediate**).
6 Jack was .... (**true**) sorry for forgetting his wife's birthday.

Past Perfect Simple

Affirmative	Negative
I **had** work**ed**	I hadn't worked
You had worked	You hadn't worked
He had worked	He hadn't worked, etc.
She had worked	**Interrogative**
It had worked	
We had worked	Had I worked?
You had worked	Had you worked?
They had worked	Had he worked? etc.

Short answers

Had I/you, etc. worked ...?	Yes, I/you, etc. had.
	No, I/you, etc. hadn't.

Use

We use **the past perfect** for:
- an action which happened before a stated time in the past.
  *He **had cooked** dinner **by six o'clock** in the evening. (He finished cooking before six o'clock.)*

- an action which happened in the past before another past action. The action which happened **earlier** is in the **past perfect**, and the action which happened **later** is in the **past simple**.
  *He **had packed** his suitcase before he **left** the house. (He packed his suitcase first and then left the house.)*

- an action which started and finished in the past and whose result was visible in the past.
  *She **had injured** her foot, so she couldn't walk.*

Time Expressions we use with the past perfect:

before, after, already, just, till/until, when, by six o'clock/midnight, etc., by the time, never, etc.

Past Perfect Continuous

Affirmative	Negative
I **had been** work**ing**	I hadn't been working
You had been working	You hadn't been working
He had been working	He hadn't been working, etc.
She had been working	**Interrogative**
It had been working	
We had been working	Had I been working?
You had been working	Had you been working?
They had been working	Had he been working? etc.

Short answers

Had I/you, etc. been working ...?	Yes, I/you, etc. had.
	No, I/you, etc. hadn't.

Use

We use **the past perfect continuous:**
- to put emphasis on the duration of an action which started and finished before a stated time in the past.
  *They **had been working** for three hours by two o'clock yesterday.*

- to put emphasis on the duration of an action which started and finished before another past action. The action which happened **earlier** is in the **past perfect continuous**, and the action which happened **later** is in the **past simple**.
  *They **had been seeing** each other for five years before they **got married**.*

- for an action which lasted for some time in the past and whose result was visible in the past.
  *She was exhausted because she **had been travelling** all night. (emphasis on duration)*

Time Expressions we use with the past perfect continuous:

for, since, how long, before, until, etc.

Must/Mustn't/Needn't: (expressing obligation/ prohibition/absence of necessity)

- We use **must** (= it is your duty to do sth, you are obliged to do sth) to express **obligation**.
  *You **must wear** a helmet when you ride a motorcycle.*
- We use **mustn't** (= it is forbidden to do sth, you are not allowed to do sth; it is against the rules or the law) to express **prohibition**.
  *You **mustn't feed** the animals in the zoo.*
- We use **needn't** (= it isn't necessary to do sth, you don't have to do sth) to express **absence of necessity**.
  *You **needn't water** the plants. I've already watered them.*

Comparative Form

- We use the **comparative form** to compare two people, animals or things. We usually use **than** with comparative adjectives. The comparative form of adjectives of three or more syllables is formed with **more**.
  *Tom is **taller than** James.*
  *This car is **more expensive than** that one.*
- We use (**not**) **as + adjective + as** to say that two people, animals or things are/are not similar.
  *My new car is **as fast as** my old one.*
  *Swimming is **not as exciting as** mountain climbing.*
- We use **less + adjective + than** for two people, things or places. It is the opposite of **more + adjective + than**.
  *I think that P.D. James' books are **less interesting than** the ones written by Agatha Christie.*

Past Perfect Simple - Past Perfect Continuous

1 Put the verbs in brackets into the past perfect or the past simple, then say which action happened first.

1 I .... (just/wake up) when someone .... (knock) on the front door.
2 I .... (have) my bus pass in my pocket but I didn't realise it .... (expire).
3 By the time she .... (reach) the harbour, the ferry .... (leave).
4 Maria .... (never/see) the ocean before she .... (leave) her village.
5 She .... (enjoy) her visit to Rome although she .... (already/go) there once before.
6 He .... (apologise) because he .... (miss) the meeting.
7 Lorna .... (look) wonderful after she .... (lose) a few kilos.
8 After they .... (finish) their picnic, they .... (take) their rubbish home with them.
9 When she .... (hang up) the phone she .... (realise) she .... (forget) to take down the caller's name and number.

10 Although I .... (set) my alarm clock, I still .... (oversleep).
11 He .... (already/pack) his suitcase before he .... (go) to bed.

2 Put the verbs in brackets into the past perfect or the past perfect continuous.

1 They .... (drive) for two hours before they finally reached their destination.
2 Emily .... (write) five letters by lunchtime.
3 The doctor told John to stay in bed until he .... (fully/recover).
4 He .... (iron) all morning when his wife arrived.
5 Peter .... (already/learn) to read and write before he started school.
6 The baby .... (cry) for half an hour before it finally fell asleep.
7 The children .... (wait) for an hour when the school bus arrived.
8 The burglar .... (get away) by the time the police arrived.
9 She .... (dig) in the garden for three hours when she stopped for a break.
10 By the time he was eighteen he .... (become) a professional athlete.
11 How long .... (they/dance) in competitions when they retired?

12 They were exhausted because they ....*had been playing*............
(**play**) chess all day.
13 A: Why were Arnold's clothes so dirty?
B: Because he ....*had*................... (**change**)
the tyres on his car.
14 By the time we joined them they .....*had*.......
..........*already*............... (**already/order**) their meal. *ordered*

3 **Fill in the gaps with the past perfect continuous of the verbs below, as in the example.**

try, walk, play, fix, work, look for

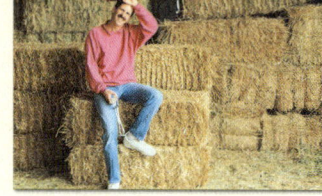

1 Kevin was confused.
He ...*had been trying*... to solve a problem for three hours.

2 Don was exhausted.
He ...*had been working hard*... hard all day.

3 Brad was desperate.
He ...*had looking for*.............. a flat for weeks.

4 Leo and Jessie were happy. They ...*had been playing*...... all afternoon.

5 Judy's feet hurt. She ...*had been walking*.... around town all morning.

6 Nick was rather tired.
He ...*had been*........ .... the computer system since eight o'clock that morning.

4 **Put the verbs in brackets into the past perfect simple or the past perfect continuous.**

1 A: Why was she exhausted?
B: Well, she ...*had been studying*......... (**study**) for hours.
2 A: Why didn't he have anything to eat at the restaurant?
B: He ...*had already eaten*........... (**already/eat**) at home.
3 A: ...*had Peter finished*............ (**Peter/finish**) cleaning the pool when you arrived?
B: No, he hadn't.
4 A: Why did they give him a promotion?
B: He deserved it because he ...*had been working*............ (**work**) hard all year.
5 A: How long ...*had they been cycling*.........
(**they/cycle**) before they stopped for a rest?
B: For five hours.
6 A: Did Frank graduate?
B: No, he didn't. Although he ...*had almost completed*............ (**almost/complete**) his studies, he dropped out in the last term.
7 A: What did you think of the modern art exhibition?
B: It was fantastic! I ...*had never seen*............ (**never/see**) such beautiful works of art before.

5 **Put the verbs in brackets into the past simple, past continuous, past perfect simple or past perfect continuous.**

A Alice **1)** ...*was*...... (**be**) very tired. She **2)** ...*had been travelling*......... (**travel**) by train for three long days and **3)** ...*had forgot*......... (**forget**) what it **4)** ...*was*............ (**be**) like to have a good night's sleep.
B Hugh **1)** ...*had*............... (**not/relax**) all week. It **2)** ...*was*............ (**be**) almost 8 o'clock on Friday morning and his physics exam **3)** ....*was*............(**be**) about to begin. Although he **4)** ...*had study*............. (**study**) hard, he **5)** ...*didn't feel*......... (**not/feel**) confident.
C It **1)** ...*was*..... (**be**) almost time. Daisy **2)** ...... (**sit**) in front of the mirror brushing her hair. As she **3)** ...*was putting*............ (**put on**) her veil she **4)** ...*had not*........ (**notice**) that her hands **5)** ...*had been trembling*........ (**tremble**). She **6)** ...*had been waiting*......... (**wait**) for this moment all her life. In less than an hour she would finally be Donald's wife.

Must/Mustn't/Needn't: (Expressing Obligation/Prohibition/Absence of Necessity)

6 **Fill in the gaps with *must*, *mustn't* or *needn't*.**

1 You .... take photos when you are in the National Museum.
2 You .... smoke when you are at a petrol station.
3 He .... come to the party if he doesn't want to.
4 You .... buy that book. I can lend you mine.
5 You .... wear formal clothes in order to attend the reception.
6 You .... go to the bank. I can give you some money.
7 You .... come in tomorrow. There's not much work to do.
8 When on a plane, you .... turn off your mobile phone.

7 **Look at the notes and make sentences using *must*, *mustn't* or *needn't*.**

(A) AT THE ZOO

1 *You mustn't feed the animals.*
2 ....
   ....
3 ....
   ....

1 feed the animals
2 use the flash when taking a photo
3 keep away from the cages

(B) AT THE THEATRE

1 ....
   ....
2 ....
   ....
3 ....
   ....

1 be seated before the play starts
2 wear formal clothes
3 smoke during the performance

(C) AT A FAST FOOD RESTAURANT

1 ....
   ....
2 ....
   ....
3 ....
   ....

1 book a table in advance
2 pay in cash
3 stay a long time

8 **Write the following sentences using *must*, *mustn't*, or *needn't*, as in the example.**

1 **It's not permitted** to walk on the grass.
   *You **mustn't** walk on the grass.*
2 **It is necessary** for John to renew his passport.
   ....
   ....
3 **It is forbidden** to park your car here.
   ....
   ....
4 **It isn't necessary** for you to come along if you don't want to.
   ....
   ....
5 **He's obliged to** be at work at six o'clock in the morning.
   ....
   ....
6 **It is forbidden** to take photos in the museum.
   ....
   ....
7 **It is your duty** to protect the environment.
   ....
   ....
8 **You aren't allowed to** use a dictionary during the exam.
   ....
   ....

33

Comparative Forms

9 Look at the pictures and the adjectives and write as many sentences as possible about the animals using *(not) as ... as*, *less ... than*, or *more ... than*, as in the example.

A)

koala bear   brown bear

big, dangerous, heavy

A koala bear is not as big as a brown bear.

B)

dog   wolf

friendly, tame, intelligent

10 Tick the correct sentence, as in the example.

1 a: A fish is less noisier than a cat. ....
   b: A fish is less noisy than a cat. ...✓...
2 a: Lions are not so big as hippos. ....
   b: Lions are not as big as hippos. ....
3 a: Going to the zoo is more entertaining watching TV. ....
   b: Going to the zoo is more entertaining than watching TV. ....
4 a: Cheetahs run faster than zebras. ....
   b: Cheetahs run as fast than zebras. ....
5 a: Was the film as exciting as the book? ....
   b: Was the film as more exciting as the book? ....
6 a: My hair is less dark than yours. ....
   b: My hair is not as dark as yours. ....
7 a: A zebra's neck is long as a giraffe's. ....
   b: A zebra's neck is not as long as a giraffe's. ....
8 a: Are dogs more loyal than cats? ....
   b: Are dogs loyal more than cats? ....

Revision: Units 1 - 6

Multiple Choice

11 Choose the correct item.

1 Angie .... abroad for four years now.
   A lived   **B** has been living   **C** lives

2 A: Where's the old lady who lives next door?
   B: She .... to Italy to visit her son.
   A has gone   **B** has been   **C** was going

3 Jane always .... home at seven o'clock in the morning.
   A has left   **B** leaves   **C** is leaving

4 Dad .... dinner while Mum was reading a magazine.
   A had cooked   **B** is cooking   **C** was cooking

5 Please be quiet! I ....!
   A work   **B** have worked
   C am working

6 A: Do you like the new restaurant?
   B: Yes, I .... there several times already.
   A went   **B** go   **C** have been

7 A: What's wrong, Dave? You look pale.
   B: I've lost a very important file .... I need for the meeting.
   A which   **B** who   **C** what

8 They .... in America for ten years.
   A was living   **B** have lived **C** are living

9 A: Why are Ann's eyes red?
   B: She .... onions!
   A chops   **B** had chopped
   C has been chopping

10 A: Have you ever worked on a farm?
    B: Yes, I worked on my uncle Tim's farm .... I was fifteen.
    A while   **B** when   **C** because

11 They .... to the theatre for ages.
    A have been   **B** aren't going **C** haven't been

12 Peggy never .... to the supermarket on Saturday.
    A goes   **B** is going   **C** has gone

Error Correction

12 Cross out the unnecessary word.

1 Did you to use to have a lot of toys when you were young?
2 The man who he lives down the street is a vet.
3 Carlos has painted a beautiful portrait of his daughter last month.
4 André was happy because he had been passed all his exams.
5 You mustn't to walk too close to the edge of the cliff.
6 The Drakes have lived here twenty years ago.

Key Word Transformation

13 Study the table, then complete each sentence with two to five words, including the word in bold.

- It is necessary to brush your teeth after meals.
  must You **must brush your teeth** after meals.
- She locked the front door, then she went to bed.
  after She went to bed **after she had locked** the front door.
- You aren't allowed to take pictures in this museum.
  mustn't You **mustn't take pictures** in this museum.
- You needn't wear formal clothes.
  necessary It **isn't necessary to wear** formal clothes.
- Pam is 165 cm. Mary is 165 cm.
  tall Pam **is as tall as** Mary.
- John is more intelligent than Harry.
  as Harry **isn't as intelligent as** John.
- The red dress costs £65, but the blue dress costs £85.
  more The blue dress **costs more than/is more expensive than** the red dress.

1 It isn't necessary for you to cook dinner tonight.
  needn't You ....
  .... tonight.
2 Ian brushed his teeth and went to bed.
  after Ian went to bed ....
  .... his teeth.
3 Kim is more hardworking than Anne.
  as Anne .... Kim.
4 Eagles are stronger than sparrows.
  not Sparrows .... eagles.
5 It is necessary to clean the cat's litter tray at least twice a week.
  must You ....
  .... litter tray at least twice a week.

6 You needn't give me a lift home.
  necessary It ....
  .... me a lift home.
7 You aren't allowed to keep library books for more than a month.
  mustn't You ....
  .... for more than a month.
8 Tom weighs 80 kilos. Bill weighs 80 kilos.
  heavy Tom ....
  .... Bill.
9 Mary's motorcycle cost £3,000, but Cathy's motorcycle cost £4,200.
  expensive Cathy's motorcyle ....
  .... Mary's.

Word Formation

> We use the following prefixes to form opposites.
> dis-   honest - **dis**honest
> il-   (before l)   legal - **il**legal
> in-   dependent - **in**dependent
> im- (before m,p) possible - **im**possible
> un-   happy - **un**happy
> ir-   (before r)   responsible - **ir**responsible
>   **But:** realistic - **un**realistic
>   reliable - **un**reliable
>   reasonable - **un**reasonable

14 Fill in the gaps with the correct words derived from the words in bold.

1 We love living in the country because life is so ..uncomplicated.. **COMPLICATED** .... here.
2 What you did was silly and ....illogical.. . **LOGICAL**
3 Mark cheated in the competition so he was ....disqualified.. **QUALIFIED**
4 Sarah was completely ..uninterested.. **INTERESTED** in what the teacher was saying.
5 The special effects in that film were very ..unrealistic.. **REALISTIC**
6 You don't need to wear a suit, it's a(n) ......informal...... party. **FORMAL**
7 This chocolate cake is ...irresistable. .... I must have another piece. **RESISTABLE**
8 It would be very ..impolite.... **POLITE** of us not to go to John's party.
9 Some of this information is ..incorrect.. . We should check **CORRECT** the facts again.
10 My dad is a shift worker. He works very ..irregular...... hours. **REGULAR**

35

Used to/Be used to/Get used to

- We use **used to + infinitive** to refer to past habits or things that do not happen any more. In such cases "used to" can be replaced by the past simple with no difference in meaning.
  *She **used to walk**/**walked** to work when she was younger. (She doesn't any more.)*
  ***Did** he **use to tell** you stories?/**Did** he **tell** you stories?*

  However, for actions which happened at a definite time in the past we use the past simple and not "used to".
  *They **went** to Jamaica last summer. (**NOT:** They ~~used to go~~ to Jamaica last summer.)*

- We use **be/get used to + noun/pronoun/-ing form** to refer to habitual actions or actions/things somebody has become accustomed to.
  Study the examples below to see how we can use **be/get used to**:

  *They **are used to cold weather**. (They are accustomed to cold weather. —present)*
  *I'm **used to going to bed** late. (I'm accustomed to going to bed late. —present)*
  *He **wasn't used to working** night shifts. (He wasn't accustomed to working night shifts. —past)*
  *Laura **is getting used to wearing** a uniform. (Laura is becoming accustomed to wearing a uniform. —present)*
  *Carol had never cooked for herself before, but she **got used to it**. (She became accustomed to it. —past)*
  *They **will** soon **get used to taking care** of their possessions. (They will become accustomed to taking care of their possessions. —future)*

Time Clauses

- Time clauses are introduced with the following time conjunctions: ***when, as, while, before, since, after, until/till, by the time, as soon as,*** etc.

  before = before a past time
  *Ann got engaged last month. Her sister had got engaged three months **before**.*

  ago = before now
  *Jason got his degree a year **ago**.*

  by the time + clause = before, not later than the moment something happens
  ***By the time** we got home, he had finished cleaning the kitchen.*

  until/till + clause/time adverb = up to the time when
  *She waited **until** the boys **had left** for school.*

  by = not later than
  *Tom must finish his project **by** Monday.*

  while/as + clause = in the time period
  *The light went out **while**/**as** I was having a shower.*

  as soon as = the moment (that)
  *We called our mother **as soon as** we arrived at our hotel.*

  when (time conjunction) + present tense
  when (question word) + will

  *I'll water the plants **when** I **get** home. (time conjunction)*
  ***When will** you be in town again? (question word)*

- Time clauses are subordinate clauses and usually go with a main clause. When the time clause precedes the main clause, a comma is used to separate the two clauses.
  After I had done the washing-up, I wrote a letter to Mum.

  time clause   main clause

- We never use future tenses after time conjunctions. We use the **present simple** or the **present perfect** instead.
  *I will relax **after I finish**/**have finished** cooking.*

  Sequence of Tenses
- Time clauses follow the rule of the sequence of tenses. That is, when the verb of the main clause is in a present or future form, the verb of the time clause is in a present form. When the verb of the main clause is in a past form, the verb of the time clause is in a past form, too.

Main Clause		Time Clause
present/future/imperative	→	present simple or present perfect
*He **brushes** his teeth **before** he **goes** to bed.*		
past simple/past perfect	→	past simple or past perfect
*Tess **had fed** the dog **before** I **got** home.*		

Used to/Be used to/Get used to

1 Fill in *used to* or the correct form of *be used to*.

1 Karen .... eating sushi because she's lived in Tokyo for years.
2 .... he .... waking up so early?
3 I .... spend my holidays in France when I was younger.
4 He .... low temperatures because he's from Sweden.
5 Beatrice .... have long hair but now she doesn't.
6 When we were children, our father .... take us sailing on Sundays.
7 He .... eat out a lot but now he enjoys cooking at home.
8 Doug and Sam............................. working hard. They never leave work before 10 o'clock at night.
9 We .... love going on picnics by the river but now we don't have the time.
10 We .... watch TV all the time but we prefer going to the cinema nowadays.

2 Fill in the gaps with the correct form of one of the verbs from the list below.

rent, have, wear, drink, live, walk, go, read

1 I used to ...*rent*... a flat but now I own one.
2 They aren't used to .... to school. Their mother always takes them in the car.
3 Is she used to .... on her own?
4 When I was a child I used to .... a lot of comics.
5 My brother and his wife used to .... on camping holidays but they don't any more.
6 He isn't used to .... a suit and tie to work.
7 My father used to .... a beard but now he only has a moustache.
8 He's not used to .... so much coffee.

Time Clauses

3 Underline the correct word(s).

1 **As soon as/Until** he had finished his lunch, he went back to work.
2 We didn't touch anything **until/as** the police arrived.
3 Please return the books **while/as soon as** you have finished with them.
4 I saw the accident **since/while** I was working in the garden.
5 **When/Since** we got home, we realised our dog was missing.
6 The taxi arrived **as/whenever** I was locking the door.
7 **After/While** he had checked into the hotel, he went to get something to eat.
8 I'd love to see you **before/by the time** you leave.
9 Can you buy me a carton of orange juice **when/until** you go shopping, please?
10 **Since/As long as** he moved to the countryside he's been more relaxed.

4 Fill in the gaps with *before, after, since, by, ago, until, by the time.*

1 I lived in San Francisco five years ....

2 .... Carol had fed the baby, she went to bed.

3 .... we reached the port, the weather had improved.

4 She bought a newspaper .... she went to work.

5 .... he's been in London he's visited the Tate Gallery and the Museum of Natural History.

6 I have to type fifteen letters .... 4 o'clock.

7 Tommy met his friends .... he had finished studying for the exam.

8 Yesterday she worked .... 7 o'clock because she was very busy.

9 How many years .... did they first meet?

10 .... we got home, the rain had stopped.

5 Match the items in Column A to those in Column B to make correct sentences, as in the example.

 **A**    **B**

1	She went to school	a	before they called a taxi.
2	They had packed their suitcases	b	they bought a farm.
3	When I saw the film star,	c	as soon as I get paid.
4	After they had sold their house,	d	the lights went out.
5	I'll go to the bank	e	after she had eaten breakfast.
6	While she was having a shower	f	I couldn't believe my eyes.

---

6 Put the verbs in brackets into the correct tense.

1 A: So what **1)** .... (you/do) until now?
 B: Well, this morning I **2)** .... (dust) the furniture and **3)** .... (sweep) the floors, and now I **4)** .... (cook) dinner.

2 A: **1)** .... (you/wash) the car today?
 B: No, I **2)** .... (wash) it yesterday.

3 A: **1)** .... (you/go) to Karen's party last night?
 B: Yes, but by the time I got there, the party **2)** .... (finish)!

4 A: So how **1)** .... (you/lose) all that money?
 B: A burglar **2)** .... (break in) and **3)** ....(steal) it while I **4)** .... (have) a bath.

5 A: How long **1)** .... (you/live) in Korea?
 B: For two years, but before that I **2)** .... (live) in Thailand.

6 A: How long **1)** .... (you/work) on the report before you **2)** .... (finish) it?
 B: For three days!

7 A: So, how often **1)** .... (you/go) swimming?
 B: I used to go every weekend but now I **2)** ...... (not/have) any free time.

8 A: Oh my goodness! Your garden **1)** .... (look) gorgeous!
 B: It should! I **2)** .... (just/ spend) three weeks working on it.

9 A: **1)** .... (you/finish) packing?
 B: Almost, but we **2)** .... (not/pack) our books yet.

10 A: When **1)** .... (you/see) your dentist?
 B: Tomorrow morning.

7 Put the verbs in brackets into the past simple, past continuous, past perfect or past perfect continuous.

A Anne **1)** .... **(drive)** along the country road enjoying the fresh air. After a while, she **2)** .... **(stop)** the car and **3)** .... **(look)** at the sea in the distance. It **4)** .... **(be)** the most beautiful view she **5)** .... **(ever/see).** After a few minutes, Anne **6)** .... **(continue)** on her way.

B Jane **1)** .... **(know)** she would be in trouble. She **2)** .... **(go)** to bed late the night before because she **3)** .... **(watch)** television. As she **4)** .... **(wait)** for the bus she **5)** .... **(wonder)** how she was going to explain to her teacher why she **6)** .... **(not/do)** her homework. She **7)** .... **(look)** at the date on her watch. "How silly of me," she **8)** .... **(think).** "It's Saturday! No school!"

Error Correction

8 Cross out the unnecessary word.

1 He was walking home when he has found a gold watch in the street.
2 I was doing the washing-up when the phone had rang.
3 Jim has often played football when he was younger.
4 We were left the party at midnight.
5 That's the woman whose her house burnt down.
6 I'll cook dinner when I will get back home.

Key Word Transformation

9 Complete each sentence with two to five words, including the word in bold.

1 She started going to the gym five weeks ago.
   since   It's been five weeks ....
                  .... to the gym.

2 When did he repair the car?
   ago   How long ....
                  .... the car?

3 It was the first time that Emily had been away from home.
   never   Emily ....
                  .... home before.

4 The last time I rode a bicycle was two years ago.
   ridden   I ....
                  .... for two years.

5 Mary didn't leave for work until she received a phone call from Sam.
   after   Mary left for work ....
                  .... a phone call from Sam.

6 She started having English lessons two weeks ago.
   been   She ....
                  English lessons for two weeks.

7 She fed the baby and then she had a cup of tea.
   soon   She had a cup of tea ....
                  .... fed the baby.

8 The last time I saw a good film was months ago.
   seen   I .... film
                  for months.

9 The teacher waited until all the students had sat down before she started the lesson.
   had   The teacher didn't begin the lesson until all .... down.

Word Formation

10 Fill in the gaps with the correct words derived from the words in bold.

Claude Monet was an artist who lived in France between 1840 and 1926. He is probably the most **1)** ~~famous~~ of all **FAME** the Impressionist painters and today visitors can see his **2)** ~~beautiful~~ **BEAUTY** paintings in museums around the world. Monet was most **3)** ~~interesting~~ **INTEREST** in painting nature scenes and his most **4)** ~~impressive~~ works are **IMPRESS** now very **5)** ~~valued~~ . However, **VALUE** at the beginning of his career, he found it **6)** ~~impossible~~ to sell any **POSSIBLE** paintings, which meant that for years he was poor. In fact, he only became very **7)** ~~successful~~ after his death. **SUCCESS** Nowadays, people can visit Monet's home and admire the **8)** ~~peaceful~~ **PEACE** gardens where he worked for much of his life.

Future Simple

Affirmative	Negative
I will work You will work He will work She will work It will work We will work You will work They will work	**I won't** work You won't work He won't work, etc.
	Interrogative
	Will I work? Will you work? Will he work? etc.

Use

We use **the future simple** for:
- predictions about the future, usually with the verbs *think*, *believe*, *expect*, etc., the expressions *be sure*, *be afraid*, etc., and the adverbs *perhaps*, *certainly*, *probably*, etc.
  *I think it **will rain** today.*
- on-the-spot decisions.
  *I'm thirsty. **I'll have** a glass of water.*
- promises, threats, warnings, requests and hopes with the verbs *promise*, *hope*, etc.
  *I **hope** the temperature **will drop** soon.*

Be going to

Affirmative	Negative
I'm going to work **You're going to work** **He's going to work** She's going to work It's going to work **We're going to work** You're going to work They're going to work	I'm not going to work You aren't going to work He isn't going to work, etc.
	Interrogative
	Am I going to work? Are you going to work? Is she going to work? etc.

Use

We use **be going to** for:
- plans and intentions we have for the near future.
  ***I'm going to spend** next summer sailing around the world.*
- predictions based on what we can see (evidence) or know.
  *The sky is very cloudy. **It's going to rain** tonight.*

Time Expressions we use with the future simple and be going to:

tomorrow, the day after tomorrow, next week/ month/ year, tonight, soon, in a week/ month/ year, etc.

Present Continuous

- **The present continuous** is used for fixed arrangements in the near future.
  *I **am seeing** my doctor next week.*

Time Conjunctions

We do not use future tenses in clauses after **while, before, until, as soon as, after, if, by the time, as**, etc.
  ***As soon as** we finish dinner, I'll serve some ice cream.*
  (**NOT:** As soon as we ~~will finish~~ ...)

Note: when (= At what time?) used as a question word can be followed by the future simple.
  ***When will** they **be** back? (when = question word)*
  *but: Susan will call us **when** she arrives. (when = time conjunction)*

Type 1 Conditionals

If-Clause (hypothesis)	Main Clause (result)
If + present simple →	will/may/can + infinitive without to

- Type 1 conditionals express a real or very probable situation in the present or future.
  *If we **leave** early, we'**ll catch** the 8 o'clock train.*
  *You **may borrow** my motorcycle if you **promise** to be careful.*
- We can use **unless** instead of *if ... **not*** in the if-clause of Type 1 conditionals. The verb is always in the affirmative after *unless*.
  ***Unless** we **leave** early, we'll miss the 8 o'clock train.*
  *(= If we **don't leave** early, we'll miss the 8 o'clock train.)*

Future Simple - Be going to - Present Continuous

1 **Fill in the gaps with the future simple or the correct *be going to* form of the verbs in brackets.**

1 They *are going to playing* (play) golf this afternoon.
2 I'm bored. I think *I'll done* (do) a crossword puzzle.
3 They are making a lot of noise. They *are going to wake* (wake) the baby.
4 You've got a bad cold. I *I'll make* (make) you some soup.
5 A: Would you like something to drink?
   B: I *I'll have* (have) a cup of tea, please.
6 We hope the dog *will find* (find) his way back home.
7 A: Look at that man on the ladder!
   B: Oh, no! He *is going to fall* (fall)!
8 A: I don't understand this Maths problem.
   B: That's OK I *I'll help* (help) you.
9 A: *Will he coming* (Alex/come) to the football match?
   B: Of course. He loves football.
10 A: Why are you wearing those old clothes?
   B: Because I *am going to paint* (paint) the kitchen today.
11 A: Mr James left a message for you. I think it's urgent.
   B: OK I *I'll ring* (ring) him right away.
12 A: Do you want to know what she told me?
   B: Oh yes! I promise I *won't tell* (not/tell) anyone else.

2 **Put the verbs in brackets into the future simple or the present continuous.**

Carla: Where 1) *are you going* (you/go) for your holidays, now that summer is here?
Erica: Nowhere. I 2) *am studying* (study) for my exams in September.

Carla: You 3) .... (not/take) a holiday at all this year then?
Erica: No. I must study, or I 4) *won't pass* (not/pass) the exams. What 5) *are you doing* (you/do) for the summer?
Carla: Well, first I 6) *am visiting* (visit) my aunt in Paris and then I 7) *am spending* (spend) a month in Antibes.
Erica: I don't really think I 8) *will have* (have) the chance to go anywhere this summer. Anyway, there's always next year, isn't there?

3 **A** **Celia Brown is the course director for an art college. Look at the prompts and say what she is going to do, as in the example.**

- design new courses
  ...*She's going to design new courses.*...
- throw a party to welcome the new students
  She is going ....
- invite artists from all over the world to give lectures
  She is going ....
- organise a workshop on local arts and crafts
  She is going to ....
- take the students on a tour of the city's museums
  She is going to ....

B **Celia is extremely busy. Look at the calendar and say what her arrangements are for the next few months. Make sentences, as in the example.**

May 15th	• fly to Florence
June 2nd	• give an interview to *Art World* magazine
25th	• have dinner with local artists
July 12th	• leave for a sailing trip
August 20th	• meet the new students at the airport

...*She's flying to Florence on May 15th.*...

Time Conjunctions

4 **Put a tick (✓) next to the sentences which are correct and cross out (✗) the unnecessary word in the sentences that are incorrect.**

1 As soon as we will reach Crete, we must try some of the local dishes. ....
2 Take the rubbish out before you will go. ....
3 After I will do my shopping, I'll have lunch with a friend. ....

4   By the time I will leave university, I'll be twenty-two. ....

5   When you see Ross, tell him I was looking for him. ....

6   If you will run into John, give him my regards. ....

7   After we finish studying, we'll go to the park. ....

8   You have to see the doctor before you will leave hospital. ....

9   When will he post the parcel? ....

10   I really don't know when he will come back. ....

5   Using the prompts and time conjunctions below, ask and answer questions, as in the example.

1   feed the cat/mop the kitchen floor - after
A: *When will you feed the cat?*
B: *I will feed the cat after I've mopped the kitchen floor.*

2   visit Aunt Bessy/finish the shopping - as soon as
A: ....
B: ....

3   have a haircut/go away for the weekend - before
A: ....
B: ....

4   vacuum the carpet/get home from work - when
A: ....
B: ....

5   take the curtains to the dry cleaner's/pick up the children from school - after
A: ....
B: ....

Type 1 Conditionals

6   First, match the prompts to the pictures. Then, make sentences, as in the example.

a)   see women wearing kimonos
b)   visit the Parthenon
c)   walk under the Arc de Triomphe
d)   admire the Taj Mahal
e)   go sailing down the Nile

Japan

India

France

Egypt

Greece

1   *If you go to Japan, you can/will see women wearing kimonos.*

2   ....

3   ....

4   ....

5   ....

7   Put the verbs in brackets into the correct tense.

1   If it ....snows........ (snow), I'll take the children skiing.

2   The football match will be cancelled if it .... (rain).

3   I won't go to the party unless Connie .... (come) with me.

4   If you .... (run) fast, you will win the race.

5   Unless they .... (work) overtime, they won't earn enough money to go on holiday.

6   .... (Greg/post) this letter for me if I ask him?

7   Unless you .... (drive) carefully, you'll have an accident.

8   If someone .... (not/water) these plants, they will die.

8 Fill in the gaps with *if* or *unless*.

1 ....*If*........... you promise to clean your room, I'll take you to the funfair.

2 I won't be able to afford a brand new car ....*unless*.... I get a loan from the bank.

3 ......*If*..... you decide to study Medicine, you'll have to work really hard.

4 ....*If*...... we win the lottery, we will travel around the world.

5 I'll never talk to you again ......*unless*...... you tell me the truth.

9 *Penny is thinking about her future.* **Look at the prompts and expand them to write Type 1 Conditional sentences.**

1 study hard/ pass exams
4 get degree/get good job
2 pass exams/ go university
5 get good job/ have a lot of money
3 do well/ university/get degree
6 have a lot of money/buy nice things

1 *If she study hers she will pass the exam,*
2 *If she pass the exam she will go to the university,*
3 *If she do well the university she we...*
4 *If she a... ...gree he will ...to a good...*
5 *If she a... ...... a she have ...*
6 *If she have a lot of money she will buy nice things*

Revision: Units 1 - 8

Key Word Transformation

10 **Study the table, then complete each sentence with two to five words, including the word in bold.**

- You will be late if you don't catch the 10.15 bus.
  unless   You will be late **unless you catch** the 10.15 bus.
- If I were you, I'd buy a cottage.
  don't   Why **don't you buy** a cottage?

1 You won't find a hotel room if you don't book early.
  unless   You won't find a hotel room ....*you do book*........... early.

2 If I were you, I would move to a better area.
  don't   Why ....*don't you move*........ ......*to a*.................. a better area?

3 You'll be late for your appointment unless you take a taxi.
  if   You'll be late for your appointment ....*if you don't take*............ a taxi.

4 Why don't you stop drinking so much coffee?
  would   If I ......*were you I'd*......... ....*stop*......... drinking so much coffee.

5 I won't go to the party if you don't come with me.
  unless   I won't go to the party ....*unless*........... ....*you come*.......... with me.

Error Correction

11 **Cross out the unnecessary word.**

1 If you ~~will~~ leave work early tonight, we can go shopping.
2 Unless he ~~not~~ calls, we'll go to his office.
3 He is ~~to~~ seeing his friends tonight.
4 ~~The~~ most of my relatives live in Portland.
5 The police took the burglars to ~~the~~ prison.

Word Formation

12 **Fill in the gaps with the correct words derived from the words in bold.**

Are you looking for a **1)** .... family car? Well, Harry's Car Dealership is the **2)** .... choice for an **3)** .... car that won't let you down. We have a wide range of **4)** .... and luxurious cars all offered at **5)** .... prices. So, come down to Harry's and get the deal of a lifetime!

RELY

SENSE

AFFORD

COMFORT

REASON

Reported Speech

- **Direct speech** is the exact words somebody said. We use quotation marks (" ") in direct speech.
  "I graduated last year," Pamela said.
- **Reported speech** is the exact meaning of what someone said, but not the exact words. We do not use quotation marks in reported speech. We can either use the word **that** after the introductory verb or we can omit it.
  *Pamela said **(that)** she had graduated the year before.*

Say / Tell

- We can use **say** and **tell** in both **direct** and **reported speech**.
- **Tell** is always used with a personal pronoun, but **say** may be used with or without a personal pronoun.
- **Say** is always followed by the preposition **to** when it is used with an object pronoun. In reported speech, **say** is not followed by an object pronoun, but it can be followed by **that.**
- We don't use **to** with **tell**.

Direct Speech	Reported Speech
*He **said**, "Jane is late again."*	*He **said** (that) Jane was late again.*
*He **said to me**, "Jane is late again."*	*He **said** (that)/**told me** (that) Jane was late again.*
*He **told me**, "Jane is late again."*	*He **told me** (that) Jane was late again.*

- **Say** and **Tell** are also used with the following expressions:

say	good morning/afternoon/evening, etc., something/nothing, etc., one's prayers, a few words, no more, so, etc.
tell	the truth, a lie, a secret, a story, the time, the difference, somebody one's name, somebody the way, one's fortune, one from another, etc.

Reported Statements

- Reported statements are usually introduced with **say (that)** or **tell (that)**.
  "He has worked for the Daily Mirror," she said. ➡ *She **said (that)** he had worked for the Daily Mirror.*
- Personal pronouns, possessive adjectives/possessive pronouns change according to the meaning of the sentence.
  "I saw a young woman running along the street," she said. ➡ *She said that **she** had seen a young woman running along the street.*

- When the introductory verb is in a past tense, the verb tenses change as follows:

Direct Speech		Reported Speech
Present Simple *"I **am** thirsty," the boy said.*	➡	**Past Simple** *The boy said (that) he **was** thirsty.*
Present Continuous *"He**'s sleeping**," she said to me.*	➡	**Past Continuous** *She told me (that) he **was sleeping**.*
Present Perfect *"I **have washed** the car," he said.*	➡	**Past Perfect** *He said (that) he **had washed** the car.*
Past Simple *"I **played** football," John said.*	➡	**Past Simple/Past Perfect** *John said that he **played**/**had played** football.*
Past Continuous *"We **were dancing** all night long," she said.*	➡	**Past Continuous/Past Perfect Continuous** *She said (that) they **were dancing**/**had been dancing** all night long.*
Future Simple *"I**'ll try** again tomorrow," he said.*	➡	**Conditional (would)** *He said (that) he **would try** again the next day.*

- The past perfect and past perfect continuous do not change in reported speech.
  *"John **had fixed** the car by the time we had dinner," she said.* ➡ *She said (that) John **had fixed** the car by the time they had dinner.*

- Certain words and time expressions change as follows:

Direct Speech		Reported Speech
• tonight, today, this week/month/year	➡	that night, that day, that week/month/year
• now	➡	then, at that time/moment, immediately
• yesterday, last night/week/month/year	➡	the day before/the previous day, the previous night/week/month/year
• tomorrow, next week/month/year	➡	the following day/the day after, the following/next week/month/year
• two days/months/years, etc. ago	➡	two days/months/years, etc. before
• here	➡	there
• come	➡	go

Tenses do not change in reported speech when:
- the introductory verb (say, tell, etc.) is in the present simple, future simple or present perfect.
  *"I **made** a cake," Grandma **says**.* ➡ *Grandma **says** that she **made** a cake.*
- the speaker reports something a short time after it was said (up-to-date reporting).
  *"The car **has broken down** again," my sister said.* ➡ *My sister said that the car **has broken down** again.*

Tenses can either change or remain the same in reported speech when the speaker reports a general truth, a law of nature or a permanent state.
*"The printing press **was invented** by Johann Gutenberg," the teacher said.* ➡ *The teacher said that the printing press **was**/**had been invented** by Johann Gutenberg.*

Reported Questions

- We introduce reported questions with **ask**, **inquire**, **wonder** or **want to know**.
- When the direct question begins with a **question word** (**who**, **where**, **how old/long**, **when**, **why**, **what**, etc.) the reported question begins with the same question word.
  *"**Where** do you live?" he asked me.* ➡ *He asked me **where** I lived.*

- When the direct question is a yes/no question and begins with an auxiliary (be, do, have) or a modal verb (can, may, etc.) then the reported question begins with **if** or **whether**.
  *"**Did** Tom go to bed late last night?" she asked me.* ➡ *She asked me **if/whether** Tom went/had gone to bed late the previous night.*

- In reported questions, the verb is in the affirmative. The question mark and words/expressions such as **please**, **well**, **oh**, etc., are omitted. Verb tenses, pronouns and possessive adjectives change as in statements.
  "Can you open the window, please?" she asked. ➡ *She asked me if/whether I could open the window.*

Introductory Verbs

To report the meaning of a speaker's words we can use various introductory verbs.

Study the examples below:

Introductory Verb	Direct Speech	Reported Speech
• **promise + to -infinitive** or **promise + that clause**	"I'll give you a lift." "I'll do my homework."	He **promised to give** me a lift. He **promised that he would do his homework**.
• **refuse + to -infinitive**	"No, I won't call Tom."	He **refused to call** Tom.
• **advise/ask + somebody + to -infinitive**	"You should take an aspirin." "Could you do something for me?"	He **advised me to take** an aspirin. He **asked me to do something** for him.
• **apologise for + gerund**	"I'm sorry I was late."	He **apologised for being/having been** late.
• **suggest + gerund**	"Let's have a picnic."	He **suggested having** a picnic.

Indirect Questions

We use **indirect questions** when we ask for information politely. Indirect questions are introduced with ***Do you know...?, Can/Could you tell me...?, Have you any idea...?, Would you mind...?*** and ***I'd like to know...*** .
The word order of indirect questions is the same as in statements (subject + verb). When the indirect question starts with ***I'd like to know***, the question mark is omitted.

Direct question: *Where is the train station?*
Indirect question: ***Do you know where the train station is?***
Direct question: *When is the next flight to Tokyo?*
Indirect question: ***I'd like to know when the next flight to Tokyo is.***

Say/Tell

1 Fill in the gaps with *say* or *tell* in the correct form.

1 Kathy ....*tell*.... her friends the truth about what had happened that night.
2 "I'll call you later," he ....*say*.... to her.
3 Ken .... us that he was having a barbecue at the weekend.
4 "Please turn the volume down," Cindy ....*said*.... .
5 "Open your books at page 29," ....*said*.... the teacher to her pupils.
6 "Could you ....*tell*.... me the time, please?" he asked me.
7 Jane ran down the stairs, ...*say*.... good morning and left for work.
8 My grandmother used to ....*tell*.... us exciting stories by the fire every night.
9 "Why did you ....*tell*....everybody my secret?" he asked.
10 "I'm sorry. I can't ....*tell*.... you the way to the station because I'm lost too," he said.

Reported Statements

2 Look at the pictures and make sentences, as in the example.

I'm looking at your plans right now, Mrs Reynolds.

1 ...*She said (that) she was looking at Mrs Reynolds' plans at that moment.*....

I've never caught such big fish before.

2 he sou that he hes never caught such a big fish before

I'll help you with the gardening, Grandmother.

3 She say that she would help her with the gardening

You can find a lot of information on the Internet, Paul.

4 She said that you could find

I can show you the road on the map.

5 she say the he can show you the road

3 Rewrite the sentences in reported speech, as in the example.

1 "There is no one at home", he said.
...*He said (that) there was no one at home.*....
2 "Mr and Mrs Wilson have gone on holiday," Mr Bradley says.
he say that they had gone holiday
3 "I'm going to the dentist now," said Lynn.
going to the dens.
4 "Jamie has never seen a dolphin before," John said.
She say that he had never seen the dolphin before
5 "I will order a pizza," he said.
he said the he would
6 "The sun rises in the east," the teacher said.
the teacher said the sun rises
7 "There was a good documentary on TV yesterday," Gregory said.
8 "It's always hot at this time of year," she said.

4 Turn the following from *direct speech* into *reported* speech, as in the example.

1 "I have a headache," she said to me.
...*She told me that she had a headache.*...

2 "I got a letter from Joanne this morning," he says.
....
....

3 "There's a bus strike tomorrow," he said to us. (up-to-date reporting)
....
....

4 "I'm going to the airport to pick up James," he said.
....
....

5 "We all speak French fluently," they said to her.
....
....

6 "I've just come back from the museum," she said to me. (up-to-date reporting)
....
....

7 "I got an A in my history test yesterday," she said to me.
....
....

8 "I've just finished reading a brilliant novel," he said to her.
....
....

Reported Questions

5 Turn the following questions from direct into reported speech, as in the example.

1 "Who broke the window?" the teacher asked the students.
...*The teacher asked the students who broke/had broken the window.*...

2 "Where are you going on holiday this year?" Josh asked me.
....

3 "What time is the wedding?" Helen asked.
....

4 "Did John go to the party last night?" Jill asked.
....

5 "Why are you laughing?" Philip asked.
....

6 "How long does it take you to walk home from here?" Peter asked.
....

7 "Will you lend me some money?" Lesley asked Sara.
....
....

8 "Who is this man?" the old lady asked her husband.
....

9 "Why did they miss their flight to Canada?" Paul asked.
....

10 "When will you visit your parents?" Sheila asked.
....

6 Turn the questions from direct speech into reported speech.

1 Do you have this in a smaller size?
....

2 Does it come in blue?
....

3 Can you order one for me?
....

4 How much does it cost?
....

5 Can I try it on?
....

6 Are there any shoes to match?
....

7 Can I pay by credit card?
....

8 When will your new stock come in?
....

Introductory Verbs

7 Complete each sentence with two to five words, including the word in bold.

1 "I'm not giving you any ice cream until you have eaten your dinner," said Barry's mother.
refused Barry's mother ...*refused to give him*... any ice cream until he had eaten his dinner.

2 "I'm sorry I broke the window," said Sean.
apologised Sean .... the window.

3 "Shall I help you carry the box?" asked Tom.
offered Tom ....
.... the box.

4 "You should tell your parents the truth," my friend said to me.
advised My friend ....
.... my parents the truth.

5 "Could you go to the bank?" he said to me.
asked   He ....
.... the bank.

6 "I really will remember to feed the fish," Maurice said.
promised   Maurice ....
.... the fish.

7 "No, I won't drive you to the football match," Mum said to me.
refused   Mum ....
.... the football match.

8 "Why don't we go to Paris for our holiday this year?" she said.
suggested   She ....
Paris for their holiday that year.

Indirect Questions

8 Complete the following indirect questions, as in the example.

1 How tall is this building?
Do you know ...*how tall this building is*...?

2 What's that girl's name?
I'd like to know ....

3 What time does the last bus leave?
Could you tell me ....?

4 How long does the flight to Rome take?
I'd like to know ....

5 How much does this dress cost?
Could you tell me ....?

6 Why was the train delayed?
I'd like to know ....

Revision: Units 1 - 9

Multiple Choice

9 Choose the correct item.

1 He said that he didn't know .... John Barry was.
A what   **B** why   **C** who

2 .... we got there, the ferry had left.
A As soon as   **B** By the time   **C** After

3 I .... the brown jacket rather than the black one, then.
A have taken   **B** will take   **C** take

4 Bob .... go fishing when he was 10 years old.
A used to   **B** got used to   **C** is used to

5 Someone .... me a very interesting story today.
A said   **B** told   **C** asked

6 In Montreal, most people speak .... French language.
A the   **B** —   **C** a

7 John promised not to .... a lie again.
A ask   **B** say   **C** tell

Key Word Transformation

10 Complete each sentence with two to five words, including the word in bold.

1 They are the people. Their daughter is a writer.
whose   They are the people ....
.... a writer.

2 He hasn't fixed the CD player yet.
still   He ....
.... the CD player.

3 The pictures were so beautiful that I bought two.
such   They were ....
.... I bought two.

4 How long is it since they bought their cottage?
ago   How ....
.... their cottage?

5 If you don't get a good night's sleep, you'll be exhausted tomorrow.
unless   You'll be exhausted tomorrow ....
.... a good night's sleep.

6 "What time does the film start on Friday night?" he asked me.
started   He asked me ....
.... on Friday night.

Error Correction

11 Cross out the unnecessary word.

1 I go for a walk in the Hyde Park every Sunday.
2 I'll tell them to call you if they will come.
3 Jo asked if that Jerry had called.
4 Can you please tell to me the way to the public library?
5 She is getting used to be studying at night.

Future Continuous

Affirmative	Negative
I **will be** work**ing**	I **won't** be working
You will be working	You won't be working
He will be working	He won't be working, etc.
She will be working	
It will be working	**Interrogative**
We will be working	Will I be working?
You will be working	Will you be working?
They will be working	Will he be working? etc.

Use

We use **the future continuous**:
- for an action which will be in progress at a stated time in the future.
  *This time next week we **will be packing** for our holiday.*
- for an action which will definitely happen in the future as the result of a routine or arrangement.
  *Don't post Ann's invitation. **I'll be seeing** her at work tomorrow, so I'll give it to her.*
- when we ask politely about someone's plans for the near future — to find out if they can do something for us.
  ***Will** you **be going** to the post office today?*

Time Expressions we use with the future continuous:

tomorrow, tonight, next week/month, etc., in two/three, etc. days, the day after tomorrow, soon, in a week/month, etc.

Future Perfect

Affirmative	Negative
I **will have** work**ed**	I **won't** have worked
You will have worked	You won't have worked
He will have worked	He won't have worked, etc.
She will have worked	
It will have worked	**Interrogative**
We will have worked	Will I have worked?
You will have worked	Will you have worked?
They will have worked	Will he have worked? etc.

Use

We use **the future perfect** for:
- an action which will be finished before a stated time in the future.
  *They **will have bought** a house by the end of this year.*

Time Expressions we use with the future perfect:

by, by the time, before, until/till, by (then), etc.

Note:
- We use the **present simple** after the time expressions **by the time, until/till, before** because they introduce time clauses.
  *By the time you **arrive**, I **will have finished** cooking.*

  time clause

  or

  *I **will have finished** cooking by the time you **arrive**.*

  time clause

- Normally, **until/till** are only used with the future perfect in negative sentences.
  *Sam **won't have fixed** the car **until** this evening.*

Linking Words / Phrases

- To add more information and/or link similar ideas we can use **furthermore, in addition, also, moreover,** etc.
  *In ten years' time, cars will be easier to drive. **Moreover,** they will be environmentally friendly.*
- To link opposing ideas we can use **but, however, on the other hand, although,** etc.
  ***Although** pollution levels have decreased, the hole in the ozone layer hasn't become smaller.*
- To express cause or reason we can use **because, as** or **since**.
  *We should take better care of our planet **because** some damage cannot be repaired.*

Future Continuous

1 Look at the pictures and use the prompts to make sentences, as in the example.

1. I/play /baseball/10 o'clock/next Saturday
   ...I will be playing baseball at 10 o'clock next Saturday....

2. At this time next month/I/ski/with my friends

3. At 2 o'clock/next Sunday/I/fish/ with my grandson

4. At this time tomorrow/we/move/ house

2 Put the verbs in brackets into the future simple or the future continuous.

Anna: Do you want to go camping this weekend?
Jan: I'd love to. I **1)** .... (call) you tonight and we can arrange everything.
Anna: Alright. Do you mind if Ellen comes with us?
Jan: Of course not. As a matter of fact, I **2)** .... (see) her for lunch so I **3)** .... (ask) her then.
Anna: OK. I **4)** .... (probably/be) home at around 8 o'clock so call me then.
Jan: Great! Just think, in three days' time, we **5)** .... (put up) our tents!
Anna: Oh yes! And we **6)** .... (sit) around a camp fire, grilling delicious fresh fish.
Jan: I can't wait!

3 Put the verbs in brackets into the future simple or the future continuous, as in the example.

1. A: Are you looking forward to your wedding?
   B: I can't wait! This time next week I *...'ll be walking...* (walk) down the aisle.
2. A: Here's the coat you wanted to borrow.
   B: Oh, thanks very much. I .... (give) it back to you on Saturday.
3. A: It's so hot!
   B: I .... (turn on) the air-conditioning.
4. A: Isn't Carol lucky? In a few weeks she .... (sail) in the Caribbean.
   B: I know! She must be excited!
5. A: .... (you/go) to the post office later?
   B: Yes, would you like me to get anything for you?
6. A: Did you tell Fred about the party?
   B: Not yet. I .... (see) him at basketball practice later on, so I .... (tell) him then.

Future Perfect

4 The people below are twenty-five years old. What do they hope they will have done by the time they are thirty years old? Using the prompts below, make sentences, as in the example.

1. Pierre: open his own restaurant
   ...Pierre hopes he will have opened his own restaurant by the time he's thirty years old....

2. Sarah: travel all over the world

3. Martin: direct a successful film

4. Alice: join a famous dance company

5 Fill in the gaps with *by the time, until, by* or *by then*, as in the example.

1 Jake will have done the shopping ...*by the time*... the children come home from school.

2 A: Have you mended my bike yet?
   B: No, I won't have mended it .... the end of the week.

3 A: Will you have booked your train ticket .... Thursday?
   B: Of course!

4 A: I won't have finished work .... 8 o'clock tonight.
   B: You poor thing. I'll have had dinner ....

5 We will have completed our project .... the end of the month.

6 Dave will have fixed the washing machine .... you get home.

6 Choose the correct item.

1 A: .... John today?
   B: Yes, why?
   A: Can you ask him if he can fix the fridge?
   A Will you be seeing   **B** Will you have seen

2 Behave yourself or else I .... you to the circus tomorrow.
   A won't be taking   **B** won't take

3 Our cherry trees .... in the spring.
   A will bloom   **B** will have bloomed

4 'Oh, Jenny, I .... lunch with Sally this afternoon. Do you want to join us?'
   A will be having   **B** will have

5 A: I'm going to invite the Johnsons over for a barbecue next Saturday.
   B: Don't bother, they .... to Paris next Saturday.
   A will go   **B** are going

6 She hopes she .... a letter from Cindy soon.
   A will receive   **B** will be receiving

7 Put the verbs in brackets into the future simple, the future continuous or the future perfect, as in the example.

1 Sally can't come to the cinema on Friday because she ...*'ll be babysitting*... (babysit) for her little brother then.

2 I ...will have finish... (finish) typing all the letters by the time Mr Howard arrives.

3 Weather forecasters predict that it ...will snow... (snow) this winter.

4 A: ...Will you be going... (you/go) to the supermarket later?
   B: Yes, why?
   A: Can you pick up some milk and eggs?

5 Don't talk so loudly, you ...will wake up... (wake up) Grandad.

6 Ashley ...will be... (be) five years old in May.

8 Put the verbs in brackets into the correct future tense.

Dear Amy,

How are you? I'm very happy because school is almost over! This time next week I **1)** ...*will be staying*... (stay) with my grandparents at their cottage by Crystal Lake.

I heard on the weather forecast that it **2)** ...will .... (probably/be) a very hot summer so I **3)** ...will be swimming... (swim) every day. My grandfather promised me that we **4)** ...will be going... (go) fishing in the lake. I can't wait!

Do you have any plans for the summer? Why don't you ask your parents if you can stay with us? I hope you **5)** ...will come... (come) to the cottage because I'm sure we **6)** ...will be having... (have) lots of fun!

Also, there is an amusement park nearby and we **7)** ...will be going... (go) there every Saturday. I am looking forward to spending a wonderful summer with my grandparents and if you come too, it **8)** ...will be... (be) even better.

Take care,
Melanie

P.S. By the time you receive this letter, I **9)** ...will have left... (leave) for the cottage. Send your reply to my grandparents' house.

Linking Words/Phrases

9 Choose the correct linking words/phrases in bold to join the sentences below, as in the example.

1 Keeping a horse as a pet is very expensive. Feeding and maintaining one costs a lot of money. **(because/furthermore)**

...*Keeping a horse as a pet is very expensive because feeding and maintaining one costs a lot of money.*...

2 Using public transport is easy and convenient. It is cheap. **(and/however)**

....
....
....
....

3 Living in a big city is stressful. It can often be unhealthy. **(also/on the other hand)**

....
....

4 Life in the future will be a lot different from how it is today. I don't think it will be exciting. **(although/ because)**

....
....

Revision: Units 1 - 10

Error Correction

10 Cross out the unnecessary word.

1 Tom is the man whose his son lives in Germany.
2 Have you still seen my wallet?
3 By the time you will finish cooking, I'll have watered the plants.
4 The phone had rang while John was having a shower.
5 Jane has been working at Madison Hospital since 1996 ago.

Key Word Transformation

11 Complete each sentence with two to five words, including the word in bold.

1 I last went to a concert four months ago.
   been   I .... concert for four months.
2 "Will you come with me?" Tom asked me.
   go   Tom asked me if ....
   .... with him.
3 "Bob and Sue will be upset if we don't invite them to our wedding", Mary says.
   unless   Mary says that Bob and Sue will be upset ....
   .... to our wedding.
4 It's not necessary to book a table in advance.
   needn't   You...
   in advance.
5 She has never seen a rainbow before.
   first   It's the ....
   a rainbow.

Word Formation

Nouns referring to people
We can form nouns that refer to people by adding -**er**, -**or** or -**ee** to the verb. build - build**er** sail - sail**or** employ - employ**ee**

12 Fill in the gaps with the correct words derived from the words in bold.

Mark's family background is very interesting. His mother is a **1)** .... and his father is an **2)** .... His older brother John is a **3)** .... His grandfather is a retired **4)** .... and his grandmother is an artist. She's a very talented **5)** .... He also has a cousin who is the **6)** .... of an international magazine. Mark and his sister Jane have more ordinary jobs. She is a **7)** .... in a law firm and he is studying to be a **8)** ....

SING
ACT
DRUM
DESIGN

PAINT
EDIT

TRAIN
TEACH

Reported Commands/Instructions/Requests

- We introduce reported **commands** or **instructions** with the introductory verbs **order** or **tell + sb + (not) to - infinitive**.
  "Don't move," she said to him. → She **ordered him not to move.**   (command)
  "Put the groceries away," she said to them. → She **told them to put** the groceries away.   (instruction)
- We introduce **requests** in reported speech with the introductory verbs **ask** or **beg + sb + (not) to - infinitive**. The direct sentence usually contains the word 'please'.
  "Please help me," Kate said to Jim. → Kate **asked Jim to help** her.
  "Please, please call an ambulance," he said to June. → He **begged June to call** an ambulance.
- In reported speech we can use a variety of introductory verbs. Study the following examples to see how these verbs are used:

Introductory Verb	Direct Speech	Reported Speech
agree **+ to - infinitive**	"Yes, I'll post the letters."	He **agreed to post** the letters.
offer	"Shall I drive you to work?"	He **offered to drive** me to work.
promise	"Of course I'll lend you the money."	She **promised to lend** me the money.
refuse	"No, I won't call her."	He **refused to call** her.
threaten	"Eat all your vegetables or I'll send you to your room."	She **threatened to send** me to my room if I didn't eat all my vegetables.
ask **+ sb + to - infinitive**	"Could you help me?"	He **asked** me **to help** him.
beg	"Please, please don't go!"	He **begged** her **not to go.**
command	"Stand to attention!"	He **commanded** the soldiers **to stand** to attention.
invite	"Would you like to have dinner with me?"	He **invited** me **to have** dinner with him.
order	"Tidy your room!"	He **ordered** me **to tidy** my room.
remind	"Don't forget to pay the bill."	He **reminded** me **to pay** the bill.
warn	"Don't skate on the lake."	He **warned** us **not to skate** on the lake.
admit (to) **+ -ing form**	"Yes, I took the money."	He **admitted (to) taking/having taken** the money.
accuse sb of	"You tore my favourite shirt."	She **accused** me **of tearing/having torn** her favourite shirt.
apologise for	"I'm sorry I forgot your birthday."	He **apologised for forgetting/having forgotten** my birthday.
complain to sb of	"I have terrible toothache."	He **complained to** me **of having** terrible toothache.
deny	"I didn't use your car."	He **denied using/having used** my car.
suggest	"Let's go for a walk."	He **suggested going** for a walk.
agree **+ that - clause**	"Yes, it's a lovely hat."	She **agreed that** it was a lovely hat.
complain	"You are always interrupting me."	He **complained that** I was always interrupting him.
deny	"I didn't break your glasses."	He **denied that** he had broken my glasses.
promise	"Of course I'll help you finish it."	He **promised that** he would help me finish it.

Reporting a Conversation/Dialogue

- We use a mixture of statements, commands and questions in conversations or dialogues. When we turn them into reported speech we use: **and**, **as**, **adding that**, **and she/he added that**, **because**, **but**, **since**, etc. We can also use introductory verbs in the present participle form (offering, begging, explaining, etc). Words or expressions such as **Oh!**, **Oh dear!**, **Well!**, etc. are omitted in reported speech.

Direct Speech	Reported Speech
"Oh! This is a fantastic painting!" she said. "Who painted it?"	*She said (that) that was a fantastic painting **and** (she) asked who (had) painted it. ("oh" is omitted)*
He took the elderly lady by the arm and said, "Can I help you cross the street?"	*He took the elderly lady by the arm, **offering** to help her cross the street.*

Reported Commands/Instructions/Requests

1 Fill in the gaps with the introductory verbs in the list in the correct form, as in the example.

order, invite, admit, threaten, deny, beg, offer, command, complain

1 "Billy, go to bed!"
Mum ...*ordered*.... Billy to go to bed.
2 "Please, please let me stay out late tonight."
Molly .... her father to let her stay out late that night.
3 "Will you come to my graduation party?"
He .... me to his graduation party.
4 "I didn't steal the sweater from the shop."
Rachel .... stealing the sweater from the shop.
5 "Put your hands in the air."
The police officer .... the robber to put his hands in the air.
6 "Stop talking or else I'll send you to the headmaster's office!"
The teacher .... to send the student to the headmaster's office if he didn't stop talking.
7 "I have an upset stomach."
He .... to me of having an upset stomach.
8 "I'll give you a lift to the train station."
He .... to give his friend a lift to the train station.
9 "Yes, I broke into the art gallery and stole the paintings."

The thief .... to breaking into the art gallery and stealing the paintings.

2 Turn the following sentences into reported speech using appropriate introductory verbs.

1 My brother said to me, "Could you help me with my Science project?"
....
....
2 My sister said, "You wore my dress without asking me!"
....
....
3 She said to me, "Don't forget to call John."
....
....
4 Rick said to Susan, "Yes, I'll pick you up at the station."
....
....
5 She said, "I really will call you as soon as I arrive."
....
....
6 He said to his mother, "No, I didn't tidy my room."
....
....
7 He said, "Shall I make you something to eat?"
....
....
8 She said to her daughter, "No, I won't buy you such an expensive watch."
....
....

9 "You're always playing your music late at night," Mr Smith said to Tom.

....

....

10 "I'm sorry I couldn't come to your wedding," Mary said to Jane.

....

....

Reporting a Conversation/Dialogue

3 Turn the following sentences into reported speech, as in the example.

1 "I'm sorry I'm late for the lesson," Sam said. "I missed the bus."
...*Sam apologised for being late for the lesson and said (that) he had missed the bus....*

2 "You'd better go to bed," Mum said. "You have to get up early tomorrow."

....

....

3 "Shall I help you with your suitcases?" Stan asked. "They look very heavy."

....

....

4 "I didn't take your wallet," Karen said. "Ben took it."

....

....

5 "Would you like to go to the opera?" Maria asked. "I've got an extra ticket."

....

....

6 "You broke the lamp," Leo said. "I saw you do it."

....

....

7 "Yes, I'll take you to the station," Dad said. "I'm going that way anyway."

....

....

8 "Please, please don't go into the house," Amy said. "There's someone in there."

....

....

9 "Don't touch the iron." Jane said. "It's very hot."

....

....

10 "Do a hundred sit-ups," the sergeant said to the soldiers. "Don't take too long, either!"

....

....

4 Turn the text below into direct speech.

Sammy asked his mother to buy him a new bike. His mother refused and said that he already had one. Sammy begged his mother and said that he wanted a mountain bike. His mother replied that Sammy didn't need a mountain bike and that his bike was fine.

Sammy: ....
Mum: ....
Sammy: ....
Mum: ....

5 Study the speech bubbles, then complete the sentences below using reported speech, as in the example.

Would you and Tom like to come to our anniversary party?

You'd better see a doctor.

I'll drive you to the airport tomorrow.

Go to your room!

Let's go to the cinema on Friday night.

Don't forget to call a plumber.

1 It was Nick and Janine's anniversary, so they ...*invited Tom and me to their anniversary party....*

2 Rachel and Sue were talking on the phone when Rachel ....

3 Stuart was leaving for Spain the following day, so Peter ....

4 The kitchen tap was dripping, so Bob ....

5 Pam broke a vase while she was playing in the living room, so her mother ....

6 Julie hadn't been feeling well for days, so Martha ....

6 Tick the correct sentence.

1 "Let's go to Venice."
   a) George suggested going to Venice.
   b) George suggested we going to Venice.
2 "You have lost the report."
   a) My boss accused me of losing the report.
   b) My boss accused on me that I lost the report.
3 "I have earache."
   a) She complained that I have earache.
   b) She complained to me of having earache.
4 "I'll buy you the doll."
   a) He promised to buy me the doll.
   b) He promised to buying me the doll.
5 "Tidy up your room!"
   a) Mum ordered me not to tidy up my room.
   b) Mum ordered me to tidy up my room.

Revision: Units 1 - 11

Key Word Transformation

7 Complete each sentence with two to five words, including the word in bold.

1 The day was so cold that we couldn't go to the park.
   such   It was ....
   .... we couldn't go to the park.
2 "Don't touch the wire!" Mum said to me.
   warned   Mum ....
   .... the wire.
3 "I'm sorry I was so rude," said Lauren.
   for   Lauren ....
   .... so rude.
4 You won't arrive on time if you don't leave early.
   unless   You won't arrive on time ....
   .... early.
5 She has never gone fishing before.
   first   It's the ....
   .... fishing.

Error Correction

8 Cross out the unnecessary word.

1 He has left for the station yet.
2 He warned at me not to play with matches.
3 It was such an awful film so that we left.
4 He has read that book last month.
5 Debra loves to listening to music.

Multiple Choice

9 Choose the correct item.

1 While Tim was reading a magazine, Sally ....
   a letter to her friend.
   A had written **B** was writing **C** has been writing
2 My sister has a friend .... speaks French fluently.
   A who   **B** whose   **C** who's
3 By the end of this week, I .... my project.
   A will finish   **B** will be finishing
   C will have finished
4 He told me .... on the grass.
   A don't walk   **B** not walk   **C** not to walk
5 Why don't you .... painting?
   A to take up   **B** taking up   **C** take up

Word Formation

We can also form nouns that refer to people as follows:
- noun/verb/adjective + **ist**   e.g. type - typ**ist**
- noun + **an/ian**   e.g. music - music**ian**
- verb + **ant/ent**   e.g. serve - serv**ant**

10 Fill in the correct word derived from the words in bold.

1 The teacher wrote the words on the board for the ....   **STUDY**
2 She asked her .... to demonstrate the new computer program.   **ASSIST**
3 Prague attracts many .... during the summer.   **TOUR**
4 Every year the company gets an .... to check their files.   **ACCOUNT**
5 Anne hired a .... to entertain the children at the party.   **MAGIC**

57

The Passive

Form

- We form the passive with the verb **to be** and the past participle of the main verb.

> **to be + past participle (pp)**

- **Study the following examples to see how the passive is formed in different tenses.**

Tense/Verb Form	Active	Passive
Present Simple	They **develop** films here.	Films **are developed** here.
Present Continuous	They **are developing** a film now.	A film **is being developed** now.
Past Simple	They **developed** this film yesterday.	This film **was developed** yesterday.
Past Continuous	They **were developing** a film when I arrived.	A film **was being developed** when I arrived.
Present Perfect	They **have** already **developed** ten films.	Ten films **have** already **been developed.**
Past Perfect	They **had developed** fifty films by two o'clock.	Fifty films **had been developed** by two o'clock.
Future Simple	They **will develop** the film tomorrow.	The film **will be developed** tomorrow.
Conditionals	They **would develop** the film if they had time.	The film **would be developed** if they had time.
Modals	They **must develop** the film by noon.	The film **must be developed** by noon.

Note: The present perfect continuous, the future continuous and the past perfect continuous are not normally used in the passive.
In colloquial English, **get** is often used instead of **be** to express something happening by accident.
*Alex **got hit** by a bus while he was cycling down the street. (= Alex was hit ...)*

Use

We use **the passive**:
- when the person who carries out the action (the agent) is unknown, unimportant or obvious from the context.
  My car was stolen last night. (unknown agent)
  The plants are watered every evening. (unimportant agent)
  The house was burgled. (by a burglar—obvious agent)
- when the action itself is more important than the agent, especially in news headlines, newspaper articles, formal notices, instructions, advertisements, etc.
  *The new wing of the hospital **was opened** by the President yesterday morning.*
- when we want to emphasise the agent.
  *The town library **was built** by my great-great-grandfather in 1874.*
- when we want to make statements more polite or formal.
  *My new CD player **is broken**. (more polite than You've broken my new CD player.)*

Changing from Active to Passive

When changing a sentence from the active into the passive:
- the object of the active sentence becomes the subject in the passive sentence.
- the active verb changes into a passive form.
- the subject of the active sentence becomes the agent and is either introduced with the preposition **by** or omitted.
- Only transitive verbs (i.e. verbs which take an object) can be changed into the passive.
  active: *Steve **wrote a letter**. (transitive verb)*
  passive: *A letter was written by Steve.*
  But: *She **came** home late last night. (The verb "come" is intransitive so the sentence cannot be changed into the passive.)*

	subject	verb	object
ACTIVE	Lisa	fed	the cat.

	subject	verb	agent
PASSIVE	The cat	was fed	by Lisa.

- **By + agent** is used to say who or what did the action.
  *The old lady was rescued **by a firefighter**.*
- **By + agent** is omitted in the passive sentence when the agent is unknown, unimportant or obvious from the context. It is also omitted when the subject of the active sentence is a word such as someone, people, I, you, etc.
  *Someone **has broken** the lock. ➡ The lock **has been broken**.*
- **With + instrument/material/ingredient** is used to say what the agent used, or after past participles such as **coloured, crowded, filled, packed**, etc.

*The omelette was made **with eggs, milk and cheese**.*
*The wood was cut **with an axe**.*
- Verbs which take two objects (**give, offer, tell, take**, etc.) can have two passive forms.
  *Mary told Kevin a secret. ➡ a) **Kevin was told** a secret by Mary. b) **A secret was told** to Kevin by Mary.*
- In the passive, the preposition that follows a verb (**accuse of, speak to, break into**, etc.) is placed immediately after the verb.
  *Dave turned the radio off. ➡ The radio **was turned off** by Dave.*
- **Let** changes to **be allowed to** in the passive.
  *Mum let us watch TV. ➡ We **were allowed to** watch TV.*

Questions in the Passive

- For questions in the passive, we follow the same rules as for statements. The verb, however, is in the interrogative form.
  *Has Anne walked the dog? ➡ **Has the dog been walked** (by Anne)?*
- When the question begins with who/what, we **cannot** omit "by".
  *Who painted the fence? ➡ Who was the fence painted **by**?*

As - Like

We use **as + noun:**
- to say what somebody or something really is.
  *He works **as** a mechanic at Ben's Garage.*

We use **like:**
- with **feel, look, smell, taste + noun**
  *It **feels** like silk.*
- with **nouns/pronouns/-ing form** to express similarity or contrast.
  *She eats **like** a bird.*
  *No one can cook **like** her.*
  *This bread is tasteless. It's **like** eating cardboard.*

The Passive

1 **Put the verbs in brackets into a suitable passive tense, as in the example.**

1 Two men ...*were seen*... **(see)** running out of the bank yesterday morning.
2 The flowers .... **(already/ water)**.
3 The Smiths' house .... **(paint)** at the moment.
4 The rubbish .... **(already/ collect)** when I left for work.
5 The note .... **(could/not/ read)** because the handwriting was very messy.
6 Our exams .... **(not/ mark)** yet.
7 His car .... **(wash)** every Saturday.
8 The window .... **(break)** before the children arrived.

59

9 The house .... **(would/sell)** if it wasn't so expensive.

10 Mary .... **(invite)** to the party but unfortunately she couldn't make it.

2 **Rewrite the sentences in the passive where possible, as in the example.**

1 Andrew cooked dinner.
...*Dinner was cooked by Andrew.*...

2 She didn't go to school yesterday.
...*It cannot be changed.*...

3 Sue painted a lovely picture.
....

4 They arrived at the airport early this morning.
....

5 Melanie posted the letter.
....

6 Bob made a fantastic puppet.
....

7 Jane left work at 8pm last night.
....

8 Joseph cleaned the fish bowl.
....

3 **Fill in the gaps with *by* or *with*, as in the example.**

1 The film was directed ...*by*... my favourite director.

2 The sauce was made .... mushrooms and onions.

3 The child was stung .... a bee.

4 The window was broken .... a piece of wood.

5 The glass bowl is filled .... fruit.

6 The dog was saved .... a neighbour.

7 The apple pie contest was won .... Mrs Jones.

8 He was shot .... a rifle.

9 They were scared .... the thunder.

10 The fingerprints on the table had been wiped off .... a towel.

11 These curtains were made .... my grandmother.

12 The cake was cut .... a knife.

13 Dan was laughed at .... his friends.

14 The house has been decorated .... balloons.

15 The parcel will be delivered .... my uncle.

4 **Put the verbs in brackets into the correct passive form, as in the example.**

1 A: Did you have a nice time in Bali?
B: Oh, yes. We ...*were taken*... **(take)** to some of the most amazing beaches I've ever seen and we ate some delicious seafood.

2 A: Did they paint their house themselves?
B: No, it .... **(paint)** before they moved in.

3 A: Where's your bicycle?
B: It .... **(repair)** at the moment.

4 A: What did you get for your birthday?
B: I .... **(give)** the most beautiful pair of earrings I've ever seen.

5 A: This bread tastes wonderful.
B: Thanks. It .... **(make)** by my mother.

6 A: When can I pick up my photos?
B: They .... **(develop)** in the morning, so any time after lunch.

7 A: That's a lovely watch.
B: It .... **(give)** to me on my retirement.

8 A: When will your car be ready?
B: I don't know. It .... **(still/fix)** when I went to the garage this morning.

9 A: Did you reserve a plane ticket?
B: No, unfortunately the flight .... **(fully/book)** by the time I got to the travel agent's.

10 A: How often should I feed the fish?
B: They .... **(must/ feed)** once a day.

11 A: A new hospital .... *is being built* (build) in our town at the moment.
   B: Yes, I know. It .... *will be opened* (open) by the mayor when it's finished.

12 A: How was the wedding reception?
   B: It was lovely! The hall .... *is decorated* (decorate) with beautiful flowers.

13 A: What's going on?
   B: A boy .... *has been trapped* (trap) in the lift and the firefighters are trying to get him out.

14 A: That was a terrible storm last night!
   B: I know. Many houses .... *were flooded* (flood).

15 A: When .... *will the report have been finished* (report/finish)?
   B: Hopefully by next week.

5 Using the prompts below, write sentences in the passive, as in the example.

1 A: Look at that house! What happened to it?
   B: It/destroy/in an earthquake.
   ...*It was destroyed in an earthquake.*...

2 A: That's a beautiful sweater you're wearing!
   B: Thank you. It/knit/my aunt.
   ....

3 A: This house is so dirty!
   B: It/not/clean/for months.
   ....

4 A: Why is John so happy?
   B: He/give/pay rise yesterday.
   ....

5 A: How's Mr Stevens?
   B: He's upset. His shop/tear down/next week/by a demolition company.
   ....

6 A: Where were you born?
   B: In Paris/but/I/raise/in London.
   ....

6 The manager of Hilltop Hotel is talking to a maid about the hotel conference room. Answer the questions using the prompts below, as in the example.

1 A: Have you vacuumed the carpets yet?
   B: Yes/the carpets/vacuum/this morning
   ...*Yes, the carpets were vacuumed this morning.*...

2 A: Have you polished the tables yet?
   B: Yes/the tables/polish/two hours ago
   ....

3 A: Have you ordered fresh flowers yet?
   B: Yes/fresh flowers/order/an hour ago
   ....

4 A: Have you cleaned the windows yet?
   B: No/the windows/clean/this afternoon
   ....

5 A: Have you dusted the chairs yet?
   B: Yes/the chairs/dust/three hours ago
   ....

6 A: Have you changed the light bulb in the cloakroom yet?
   B: No/the light bulb in the cloakroom/change/later this afternoon
   ....

7 Rewrite the following in the passive.

1 Who invented the telephone?
....

2 The thief stole all the money in the till.
....

3 Who has written this poem?
....

4 When will they hold the annual dance?
....

5 Many tourists visit the Eiffel Tower every year.
....

6 Did you give the parcel to Susie?
....

7 The fire damaged many buildings in the city centre.
....

61

8 The repairman is fixing the washing machine.

The washing machine is being fixed by the repairman

9 Has Victoria sent out the invitations?

Have the invitations been sent out by her?

10 They will open the new library to the public in September.

....

11 We took many of these photographs when we were in India.

....

12 They will dedicate the new university building to Dr Peters.

....

13 Will she redecorate her flat in May?

Will that flat be redecorated

14 Dora sold three sculptures at the gallery opening.

....

15 Who made this delicious chocolate cheesecake?

Who ate the delicious chocolate cheesecake? By whom was this delicious chocolate cheesecake made by

8 Rewrite the following passages in the active or passive, accordingly.

A Rosemary Hills train station was built by Sean Carlton and his wife Sharon in 1894. For the construction of the waiting room, red brick had been imported from England by the Carltons. The station was opened in 1896 by the President himself. That year, Rosemary Hills was visited by a steam locomotive for the first time. It was pumping clouds of white smoke and whistling loudly enough to be heard by all the townspeople.

Sean Carlton and his wife Sharon built Rosemary Hills train station 1894. For the construction of the waiting room, the Carltons had imported red brick from England...

B The news reporter announced that the police are looking for a man who broke into the National Bank. The thief cut the wires of the alarm and then broke into the bank's city centre branch some time late last night. The thief stole £500,000 from the bank. The police are searching the city centre as they believe the thief is still in the area.

....
....
....
....
....
....
....

As - Like

9 Fill in the gaps with *as* or *like*, as in the example.

1 The clouds in the sky look ...*like*... cotton.
2 Mr Samson works .... a slave.
3 Paula would like to find a job .... a newspaper journalist.
4 Mr Hart works .... a professor at Oxford University.
5 Mary and her sister fight .... cat and dog.
6 She has been working .... a vet for a year.
7 "What are you cooking? It smells .... fish."
8 "Sammy, you're a big boy now. Stop acting .... a baby," she said.
9 Mrs Madison was offered a job .... a sales assistant in a nearby boutique.
10 Mr Petroni is looking for a job .... a chef in an Italian Restaurant.
11 Carol has got a mobile phone .... mine.
12 Their news came .... a complete surprise to everyone who knew them.
13 "The sky is very dark."
   "Yes, it looks .... rain."
14 That child behaves .... an angel.
15 No one can sing that song .... him.

Revision: Units 1 - 12

Multiple Choice

10 Choose the correct item.

1 Carla always .... early on Sunday mornings.
   A gets up   **B** get up   **C** getting up

2 John .... a shower at the moment.
   A has   **B** have   **C** is having

3 That's the little boy .... lost his dog.
   A who   **B** whose   **C** which

4 Gary has been travelling .... August.
   A for   **B** since   **C** until

5 It was .... a horrible day that we stayed at home.
   A —   **B** so   **C** such

6 Did Sarah .... drink a lot of milk when she was young?
   A use to   **B** used to   **C** using to

7 We .... to the beach yet this summer.
   A haven't been   **B** didn't go   **C** haven't gone

8 Jim is looking for a job .... a personal assistant.
   A as   **B** like   **C** such

9 He .... me about the concert last night.
   A said   **B** ordered   **C** told

10 You'll fail your exams .... you study.
   A when   **B** unless   **C** if

Key Word Transformation

11 Complete each sentence with two to five words, including the word in bold.

1 Steven Spielberg directed *ET: The Extraterrestrial*.
   was   *ET: The Extraterrestrial* ....
   .... Steven Spielberg.

2 "Don't touch the iron!" said Mum.
   warned   Mum ....
   .... the iron.

3 It was so cloudy that we didn't go to the beach.
   such   It ....
   .... that we didn't go to the beach.

4 You can't go to the basketball game tonight if you don't finish your homework.
   unless   You can't go to the basketball game
   tonight ....
   .... your homework.

5 John's watch cost £30, but Mike's watch only cost £25.
   expensive John's watch was ....
   .... Mike's.

6 Vicky started taking violin lessons four years ago.
   has   Vicky ....
   .... for four years.

7 The bakery is next to my house. It sells delicious bread.
   which   The bakery ....
   .... my house sells delicious bread.

8 Have you told all the employees that there will be a meeting tomorrow morning?
   been   Have ....
   .... that there will be a
   meeting tomorrow morning?

Error Correction

12 Cross out the unnecessary word.

1 We went to the Amsterdam for two weeks last summer.
2 This song it is expected to reach number one in the top ten.
3 The dog that it bit me is my neighbour's.
4 She told to me she would be late.
5 He suggested that they should to leave early.
6 She told us do not to touch the wire.
7 He promised that to be back early.
8 I have read this book last summer.

Word Formation

13 Fill in the correct word derived from the word in bold.

Dear Jenny,

How are you? Ray and I arrived in Dolphin Bay yesterday. We are staying at a **1)** .... campsite, only five minutes from the beach. The weather has been hot and **2)** ....

It is very **3)** .... here as there are no cars. The quiet environment makes me feel very **4)** .... It is my first time camping and I never thought I would like it this much. I'm having a great time.

There is a restaurant on the campsite which serves very **5)** .... food. Just thinking about it makes me **6)** .... !

See you soon,
Nancy

MARVEL

SUN

PEACE

RELAX

TASTE
HUNGER

Need

- We use **need** and an **-ing form** or a **passive infinitive** to show that it is necessary to improve or repair something.
  e.g. *The windows* **need cleaning**.
  The windows **need to be cleaned**.

Personal/Impersonal Construction

- The verbs **think**, **believe**, **say**, **report**, **know**, **expect**, etc. are used in the following passive patterns in personal and impersonal constructions.

active	→	*People* **say** *that he* **has won** *the lottery.*
passive	→	a) *It is said (that) he has won the lottery. (impersonal construction)*
		b) *He is said to have won the lottery. (personal construction)*

active	→	*People* **expect** *that Sue Peters* **will break** *the world record.*
passive	→	a) *It is expected (that) Sue Peters will break the world record.*
		b) *Sue Peters is expected to break the world record.*

active	→	*People* **believe** *that he* **sold** *the painting.*
passive	→	a) *It is believed (that) he sold the painting.*
		b) *He is believed to have sold the painting.*

Need

1 Look at the sentences and rewrite them in the need + ing form and the need + passive infinitive form using the words in bold, as in the example.

1 The baby is hungry. **(feed)**
   ...*The baby needs feeding*....
   ...*The baby needs to be fed*....

2 The car has a flat tyre. **(change)**
   The car need to be changing

3 Your room is a mess. **(tidy)**
   Your room need tidying

4 The plants are dry. **(water)**
   the plant need watering

5 The dog is barking. **(walk)**
   need walking

6 This shirt is wrinkled. **(iron)**
   The shirt need ironing

7 Your nails are too long. **(cut)**
   Your nail need cutting

8 The radio is broken. **(fix)**
   the radio need fixing

9 The petrol tank is empty. **(fill)**

10 Your blouse is torn. **(sew)**

11 The rubbish bin is full. **(take out)**

12 The batteries are dead. **(charge)**

13 Your hair looks terrible. **(brush)**

14 This pencil is blunt. **(sharpen)**

15 The lights are off. **(turn on)**

16 The letters are ready. **(post)**

Personal/Impersonal Construction

2 **Rewrite the following sentences in the passive using personal and impersonal constructions, as in the example.**

1 People say that she has millions in the bank.

It ...*is said (that) she has millions in the bank.*...

She ...*is said to have millions in the bank.*...

2 The newscaster reported that the President resigned last night.

It ...... *is reported that the President* ......

....

The President ...... *is reported to have*

...... *resigned last night* ......

3 People believe that an electrical problem caused the fire.

It ...... *is believed that* , ...

....

An electrical problem ...... *is believed to*

have caused the fire ......

4 Everyone thinks that he stole the money.

It ...... *is thought that he stole*

the money ......

He ...... *is thought to have stolen*

the money ......

5 People know that she has lived in many countries.

It ...... *is known that she* ......

....

She ...... *is known to have*

lived in many countries ......

6 People expect that he will win an award.

It ...... *is expected that he will* ......

....

He ...... *is expected to win*

it an award ......

3 **Underline the correct form of the verbs, as in the example.**

A: How was your first day in your new job?

B: Oh, quite good really, although it **1) started**/had started badly because my car **2) had broken down/broke down** on the way.

A: Oh dear. Were you late?

B: No. Fortunately, I **3) was given/gave** a lift by my brother.

A: So what happened when you got there?

B: Well, I **4) reported/was reporting** to my manager and then she **5) was introducing/introduced** me to everyone and I **6) was shown/showed** my desk. Then, the phone **7) had started/started** ringing and never stopped. I was very busy all day.

A: **8) Did you have/Were you having** any problems?

B: Not really. Everyone was really nice. I **9) had/ was having** a problem with the coffee machine, though.

A: Don't tell me you **10) broke/had broken** it!

B: Yes. How did you guess? I **11) was putting/put** my money in when it **12) made/was making** a strange noise. Then, the coffee **13) poured/was pouring** out all over the floor! It **14) had broken/ was broken** the day before and they **15) had forgotten/have forgotten** to tell me!

4 Match the people's comments with the natural disasters, then rewrite their words in the passive, as in the example.

volcanic eruption, earthquake, avalanche, fire, tornado, flood

> Experts had predicted the eruption weeks before.

> Ten metres of snow buried a village north of Montreal.

1 ...*volcanic eruption: The eruption had been predicted weeks before.*...

2 ....
....
....
....

> Rescue workers have pulled out three people from under the debris.

> The violent winds destroyed many houses in the area.

3 ....
....
....
....

4 ....
....
....
....

> It will burn hundreds of acres of forest.

> They are sending tents to shelter people because the water has swept their houses away.

5 ....
....
....
....

6 ....
....
....
....

5 Rewrite the following passage in the passive.

Late last night, two boys broke into the *Lots and Lots of Toys* store on Park Avenue. An employee had left a small window open. Police believe that the boys climbed in through the window. They stole £2,500 worth of toys. The police have not found the boys yet.

....
....
....
....
....
....
....
....

6 Put the verbs in brackets into the correct active or passive tense, as in the example.

Ice cream, one of the most favourite desserts in the world, **1)** ...*was introduced*... **(introduce)** to Europe from the East. In 1670, Francisco Procopio opened a café in Paris, serving ices and sherbets. The ices and sherbets **2)** .....*became*..... **(become)** so popular that by 1676 there **3)** ...*were*...... **(be)** 250 ice makers in Paris. However, another café owner in Paris in the late 18th century by the name of Tortoni **4)** ....*said*...... **(say)** to be the first person to make cream ices. The main ingredients which **5)** ....*were*......... **(use)** to make ice cream **6)** .....*were*........... **(be)** milk, cream, sugar and eggs. These ingredients **7)** .....*were combined*........... **(combine)** to make a mixture which **8)** ......*was put*...... **(put)** in a large container and **9)** ....*refrigerated*...... **(refrigerate)** for several hours. Then, chopped nuts or chocolate pieces **10)** .....*added*............. **(add)** to make different flavours. After that, the ice cream **11)** .....*was packed*....... **(package)** individually and finally it **12)** ....*frozen*........ **(freeze)**.

People of all ages **13)** ....*love*....... **(love)** eating ice cream. It **14)** ....*is*.......... **(be)** a wonderful treat, especially when it **15)** .....*topped*...... **(top)** with delicious syrups and whipped cream!

Revision: Units 1 - 13

Multiple Choice

7 Choose the correct item.

1 Tanya has been exercising .... 9.00 this morning.
A since   **B** for   **C** at

2 It was .... beautiful painting that I bought it.
A such   **B** so   **C** such a

3 If you're not on time, we .... without you.
A leave   **B** will leave   **C** will have left

4 A meeting .... once a month.
A have been held   **B** is holding   ~~**C** is held~~

5 Ellen works .... a waitress at *Gustav's*.
A like   **B** as   **C** such

6 The fish .... feeding.
A need to be   **B** need to   **C** need

7 "The bus .... an hour ago," the man said.
A was leaving   **B** left   **C** has left

8 A: Shall I buy some more bread?
B: No, I .... some yesterday.
A have bought   **B** bought   **C** buy

Error Correction

8 **Cross out the unnecessary word.**

1 My brother said that he couldn't ~~to~~ drive me to school.
2 Lisa ~~has~~ rarely goes to the beach.
3 He told us ~~do~~ not to tell lies.
4 We arrived after the film had ~~been~~ started.
5 She's been cooking all ~~the~~ day.

Key Word Transformation

9 **Complete each sentence with two to five words, including the word in bold.**

1 It's two years since Bessie has been on holiday.
for   Bessie has .... two years.
2 "I'm sorry for not returning the book on time," she said.
apologised She .... the book on time.
3 It's the first time he has ridden a horse.
never   He .... before.
4 Why don't you get a guard dog?
would   If .... get a guard dog.
5 They won't let you in if you don't have a ticket.
unless   They will .... you have a ticket.
6 "Don't play near the train tracks," she said to us.
warned   She .... near the train tracks.

7 They are sending an ambulance to the scene of the crash.
being   An ambulance .... the scene of the crash.
8 It was so hot that we couldn't sleep that night.
such   It was .... we couldn't sleep.
9 "I am writing a book," Tim said to me.
told   Tim .... writing a book.
10 They found the puppy under the sofa.
was   The puppy .... the sofa.

Word Formation

> We form nouns from adjectives by adding:
>
> **-ance**   *e.g. arrogant - arrog**ance***
> **-ence**   *e.g. intelligent - intellig**ence***
> **-ness**   *e.g. polite - polite**ness***
> **-ity**   *e.g. active - activ**ity***
> **-ty**   *e.g. cruel - cruel**ty***
> **-y**   *e.g. jealous - jealous**y***

10 **Fill in the gaps with the correct words derived from the words in bold.**

1 Matthew has .... reading without his glasses.   **DIFFICULT**
2 Great .... is placed on experience in this company.   **IMPORTANT**
3 Sharon showed her .... by moving into her own flat.   **INDEPENDENT**
4 It was the mayor's .... that helped him win the election.   **POPULAR**
5 Paul and Danielle's .... made Adrian jealous.   **HAPPY**
6 All toys should be checked for ....   **SAFE**
7 Fran's .... always made her blush in public.   **SHY**

Type 2 Conditionals - unreal present

- Type 2 conditionals are used to express **imaginary** or **improbable situations**, which are unlikely to happen in the **present** or **future**.

if - clause (hypothesis)	main clause (result)
if + past simple	**would/could/might + bare infinitive**

*If I **had** a lot of money, I **would buy** a house in Monte Carlo. (But I don't have a lot of money. Here, we refer to the present.)*
*If my car **broke down**, I **would take** the bus. (But I don't expect my car to break down. Here, we refer to the future.)*
- We use **if + were** to give advice:
*If I **were** you, I **would talk** to my parents.*
- We can use **were** instead of **was** for all persons in the if-clause.
*If he **were/was** here, he would help us solve the problem.*

Type 3 Conditionals - unreal past

- Type 3 conditionals are used to express **imaginary** or **improbable situations** which never happened in the **past**. They are also used to express regret or criticism.

if - clause (hypothesis)	main clause (result)
if + past perfect	**would/could/might + have + past participle**

*If I **had known** that Stanley was in town, I **would have invited** him to the party. (But I didn't know that Stanley was in town, so I didn't invite him to the party.)*
*If we **had arrived** at the theatre earlier, we **would have found** a seat. (But we didn't, so there weren't any seats left.)*

Wishes

- **Wish/If only + subject + past simple** is used to express wish/regret about a **present situation**.
*I **wish/If only** I **knew** where she lived.*
(I'm sorry (that) I don't know where she lives.)
*I **wish/If only** I **were** taller. (But I am not.)*
- We can use **were** instead of **was** for all persons.
- **Wish/If only + subject + past perfect** is used to express regret about a **past situation**. (something that happened or didn't happen in the past.)
*I **wish/If only** I **hadn't lied** to him. (I'm sorry (that) I lied to him.)*

Linking Words/Phrases

- We can use **also, in addition to this, what is more, furthermore, moreover, besides this**, etc. to add more information and/or link similar ideas.
*Being a journalist is an exciting job. **Besides this**, you get to travel all over the world.*
- We can use **however, on the other hand, nevertheless, although, in spite of the fact (that), despite the fact (that), in spite of, despite, yet, but**, etc. to link contrasting ideas.
*Being a doctor is a well-paid job. **However**, it is very hard work.*

Type 2 Conditionals

1 Match the items in column A with those in column B to make sentences, as in the example.

A	B
1 If I were you,	**a** we would see each other more often.
2 If Sara lived near me,	**b** he would donate some to charity.
3 If Peter had a lot of money,	**c** I would do more exercise.
4 If Dad didn't have to work today,	**d** he could take us to the zoo.

2 Put the verbs in brackets into the correct tense, as in the example.

1 If Steven ...*had woken up*... **(wake up)** half an hour earlier, he wouldn't have been late for work.
2 If I .... **(be)** you, I would study Law.
3 If I were a doctor, I .... **(work)** for the organisation *Doctors without Borders*.
4 If Mary had enough money, she .... **(open)** her own restaurant.
5 If George .... **(know)** her name, he would tell me.
6 If we had a car, we .... **(drive)** across the USA.

Type 3 Conditionals

3 **Read the story below and make Type 3 conditional sentences, as in the example.**

Carl had a horrible camping trip last weekend. He woke up late, so he had to rush. He forgot to pack his sleeping bag, so he slept on the cold, hard ground. He didn't take any insect repellent, and as a result he was bitten by mosquitoes. It rained on Sunday, so he left early.

...If Carl hadn't woken up late, he wouldn't have had to rush.... ~~if he had taken an insects repellent he wouldn't have been bitten by mosquitoes~~

....
....
....
....
....

4 **Put the verbs in brackets into the correct tense.**

1 A: If you .... **(go)** to the supermarket, ... **(you/buy)** some milk, please?
B: Of course. ~~will~~

2 A: I haven't been feeling well lately.
B: If I .... **(be)** you, I .... **(call)** the doctor's for an appointment.

3 A: Mum, I didn't pass the Maths test.
B: If you .... **(study)** for it, you .... **(pass)** it.

4 A: What time should I expect you?
B: If the bus .... **(come)** on time, I .... **(arrive)** around 3.00.

5 A: I can't believe that people still drop litter!
B: I know! If everyone .... **(stop)** dropping litter, our neighbourhood .... **(be)** a nicer place to live in.

6 A: If you .... **(see)** Bill, can you tell him to call me?
B: Of course.

7 A: Will you come to the cinema with me?
B: I'm sorry but I'm busy. If I .... **(not/have)** so many things to do at home, I .... **(come)** with you.

8 A: Dad, why didn't you let me play with Annie yesterday?
B: If you .... **(finish)** your homework, you .... **(play)** with her.

9 A: Do you live in Paris?
B: No, but if I .... **(live)** in Paris, I .... **(learn)** to speak French fluently.

Wishes

5 **Rewrite the following sentences to express either *an unreal situation in the present* or a *regret about a past event*.**

1 I scratched my sister's favourite CD.

...I wish I hadn't scratched my sister's favourite CD. (regret)...

2 I haven't got a motorcycle.

...I wish I had a motorcycle. (unreal situation)...

3 I am not old enough to go to nightclubs.

....

4 I left school without any qualifications.

....

5 I missed the plane to Lisbon.

....

6 I am not tall enough to join the basketball team.

....

7 I didn't call my grandfather last night.

....

8 I forgot my parents' anniversary.

....

6 Make sentences, as in the example.

1 have a job/not feel bored

...I wish I had a job. If I had a job, I wouldn't feel bored....

2 have customers/be busy

I wish I had customers. If there was customer I will be busy

3 know the answers/ be able to pass the exam

I wish I know if know the I will b able to pass the exam

4 have some help/ finish quicker

I wish I be some help it I have some help I will finish quicker

5 have a hat/not be so hot

I wish I had what hat If I have a hat I won't be you so hot

6 own a camera/take a picture

I wish she had own a camera If I own a camera I take great picture

7 Put the verbs in brackets into the correct tense, as in the example.

1 If I *...were...* (be) you, I would tell him the truth.
2 I wish I *hadn't forget* (not/forget) my keys. Now I can't get into my house.
3 If he were faster, he *would* (win) the race.
4 I wish I *hadn't* (not/eat) all those sweets. Now I feel sick.
5 If she *finding* (find) a kitten, she'll keep it.
6 If I *have* (have) a garden, I would grow my own vegetables.

7 I wish you .... (listen) to me. If you had listened to me, you .... (not/lose) your job.
8 If you continue to eat junk food, you .... (gain) weight.

8 Look at the pictures, then use the prompts to make Type 2 or 3 conditional sentences.

1 it/snow/last weekend/we/ go skiing

....
....
....

2 she/learn/to sew/she/ make/her own clothes

....
....
....

3 Tom/have/bicycle/he/ cycle/to work /every day

....
....
....

4 It/be/Johnny's birthday/ they/have/a party

....
....
....

9 Continue the sentences, as in the example.

1 If I had a lot of money, *...I would travel around the world....*
2 If you go to the gym every day, ...
3 If you touch the hot iron, ...
4 If Sally had passed her exams, ...
5 If Fred had a summer house, ...
6 If I hadn't woken up late, ...
7 Unless you call her, ...
8 If they had invited him to the picnic, ...

Linking Words/Phrases

10 Underline the correct linking word/phrase, as in the example.

1 He was exhausted, **as well**/<u>yet</u> he took the dog for a walk.
2 **However/Despite** being short, he's an excellent basketball player.
3 **Even though/But** they are poor, they are very generous.
4 **On the other hand/In spite of** being qualified, she can't find a job.
5 **Despite the fact that/Also** she can't sing well, the band still hired her as their singer.
6 It's a dangerous job. **Moreover/Nevertheless**, the pay is extremely good.

Revision: Units 1 - 14

Multiple Choice

11 Choose the correct item.

1 He was making a cake .... his wife called.
   A as   **B** because   **C** when

2 The Clarks .... a new refrigerator last month.
   A bought   **B** are buying   **C** buy

3 They .... shopping last night.
   A weren't going **B** didn't go **C** haven't gone

4 The sun .... in the west.
   A is setting   **B** sets   **C** set

5 If we .... early, we'll get a good seat.
   A are leaving **B** left   **C** leave

6 Annie .... me that she was moving to Alaska.
   A told   **B** told to   **C** said

Error Correction

12 Cross out the unnecessary word.

1 Simon won't have been fixed the roof until tomorrow morning.
2 They are to leaving for the seaside this evening.
3 I am reading a book which it is extremely interesting.
4 She was be watching TV when the lights went off.
5 If I was won the lottery, I would buy a yacht.

Key Word Transformation

13 Study the table, then complete each sentence with two to five words, including the word in bold.

1 She was exhausted, yet she still went out with her friends.
   being   Despite ...., she still went out with her friends.
2 I'm sorry I wasn't at your wedding.
   wish   I .... your wedding.
3 I last went to the cinema six months ago.
   been   I .... cinema for six months.
4 Despite having studied for the exam, she didn't pass it.
   had   Although .... the exam, she didn't pass it.
5 "Don't go near the edge of the pool," she said.
   warned   She .... near the edge of the pool.
6 It's not necessary for you to call me before you leave.
   need   You .... before you leave.

Word Formation

14 Fill in the gaps with the correct words derived from the words in bold.

I love my job even though it's **1)** .... There are a lot of risks involved but it's also very **2)** .... In the past, it was quite **3)** .... to see a woman firefighter and when I was a **4)** ...., there were hardly any at all. It was thought that women would have **5)** .... in doing this kind of job, but we have proved everyone wrong. Despite the fact that it is hard work and quite tiring, firefighting is an **6)** .... job. I have been a firefighter for years and I have never felt **7)** .... Everyone I work with finds it an **8)** .... career to have and they **9)** .... agree with me that being a woman is not a **10)** .... in becoming a firefighter.

DANGER
REWARD
USUAL
TRAIN
DIFFICULT
INTEREST
BORE
ENJOY
CERTAIN
ADVANTAGE

The to-infinitive

We use the **to-infinitive**:
- to express purpose.
  *She went to the chemist's **to buy** some aspirin.*
- after **would love**, **would like**, **would prefer**.
  *I'd **love to see** the Taj Mahal one day.*
- after certain adjectives such as: **glad, difficult, happy, sorry, willing**, etc.
  *We were **glad to help** them fix their roof.*
- after certain verbs such as: **advise, agree, appear, decide, expect, hope, learn, manage, offer, promise, refuse, seem, teach, want**, etc.
  *We can't **decide** where **to eat** tonight.*
- in the expressions: **to tell (you) the truth, to begin with, to be honest, to start with, to sum up**, etc.
  ***To be honest**, I hate watching horror films.*
- after **too** and **enough**. *This curry is **too** spicy for me **to eat**.*

The Infinitive without to

We use the **infinitive without to**:
- after modal verbs: **can, could, may, might, will, would, must**, etc.
  *You **must call** your mother immediately.*
- after the verbs **feel, hear, make, let, see**.
  *She **made** him **clean** his room.*
But: be made/be heard/be seen + to-infinitive
  *He **was made to clean** his room.*

The -ing form

We use the **-ing form**:
- as a noun.
  ***Smoking** is forbidden in this building.*
- after **love, like, dislike, hate, enjoy, prefer**, etc.
  *I **love watching** the sun set every evening.*
- after prepositions.
  *They left **without taking** their change.*
- after certain verbs such as: **avoid, admit, fancy, finish, forgive, imagine, keep (=continue), mind (=object to), regret, suggest**, etc.
  *They **suggested eating** at the local Italian restaurant.*

- after the expressions: **I'm busy, it's no use, it's (not) worth, what's the use of, can't help, can't stand, there's no point (in), look forward to, what about ...?, how about ...?**, etc.
  ***It's no use calling** him. He can't hear.*

Certain verbs may be followed by **either** the **to-infinitive** or the **-ing form**. In this case, however, there is **a change in meaning.**

Forget
forget + to-infinitive = not remember
*I'm sorry I **forgot to call** you.*
forget + -ing form = forget a past event
*I will never **forget meeting** the President.*

Remember
remember + to-infinitive = not forget
*She **remembered to lock** the door.*
remember + -ing form = recall a past event
*I don't **remember turning off** the TV.*

Try
try + to-infinitive = do one's best, attempt
*The divers **tried to find** the sunken treasure but they couldn't.*
try + -ing form = do sth as an experiment
***Try going** to bed earlier. You might feel better.*

Stop
stop + to-infinitive = stop for a while in order to do sth else
*She **stopped to eat** a sandwich and then continued studying.*
stop + -ing form = finish, end
*He **stopped drinking** coffee because it keeps him awake.*

Regret
regret + to-infinitive = be sorry
*We **regret to inform** you that Flight 714 to Boston has been cancelled.*
regret + -ing form = have second thoughts
*I **regret shouting** at him that way.*

Note: the verbs **hear, see, watch, notice** and **similar verbs of perception** can be followed by:

object + infinitive without to or **object + ing form**

*I **saw him cross** the bridge. (= As I looked, he crossed it from one side to the other.)*
*I **saw him crossing** the bridge. (= As I looked, he was crossing it — he was in the middle, on his way across.)*

The to-infinitive/The Infinitive without to/ The -ing form

1 Say whether the words/expressions below are followed by the a) to-infinitive, b) infinitive without to, c) -ing form, as in the example.

1 hope ...*a*...
2 make ....*b*
3 can't stand ...*c*.....
4 let ....*b*...
5 love ....*c*
6 promise ....*a*
7 it's not worth ....*c*
8 want ....*a*
9 decide .....*a*....
10 can't .....*b*..
11 look forward to ...*c*...

12 refuse ....*a*
13 there's no point (in) .... *c*
14 might ....*b*
15 hear ....*b*
16 offer ....*a*
17 seem ....*a*
18 glad ....*a*
19 how about ....*c*
20 must ...*b*....

2 Fill in the gaps with the verbs in brackets in the correct form of the infinitive or -ing form, as in the example.

1 A: Is Ed in his room?
   B: Yes, I can hear him ...*talking*... **(talk)** on the phone.
2 A: Did the police catch the robber?
   B: Yes. He admitted ...*robbing*... **(rob)** the jewellery shop.
3 A: Do you want to rent *Rambo* tonight?
   B: No. I can't stand ...*watching*... **(watch)** violent films.
4 A: Is everything ready for the party tomorrow?
   B: Yes, almost. I've decorated the house, but I forgot ...*to buy*... **(buy)** some balloons.
5 A: When will Adam return the lawnmower?
   B: He will ...*return*... **(return)** it on Saturday.
6 A: What time is it?
   B: It's half past eight. You'd better hurry or you'll ....*miss*... **(miss)** the bus.
7 A: What did Mr Jones say?
   B: He advised me ....*to speak*... **(speak)** to a lawyer.
8 A: What time do you have to go home on Friday nights?
   B: My parents let me ....*stay*... **(stay)** out until eleven o'clock on Fridays.
9 A: Do you like living in Alaska?
   B: Alaska is beautiful, but I can't get used to ....*living*.... **(live)** in such cold weather.
10 A: How often do you clean your room?
    B: My mother makes me ....*clean*... **(clean)** it every week.

3 Fill in the correct form of the verbs in brackets (to-infinitive or -ing form), as in the example.

1 I'll never forget ...*meeting*... **(meet)** Sharon Stone.
2 I regret ....*to inform*......... **(inform)** you that you didn't pass the exam.
3 Do you remember ....*seeing*... **(see)** this film?
4 I forgot ....*to add*......... **(add)** milk so the sauce is ruined.
5 Alan stopped ....*taking*............ **(take)** taxis to work because it was too expensive.
6 The archaeologist tried ....*to find*......... **(find)** the lost city but she had no luck.
7 He always remembered ....*to water*......... **(water)** the plants before he left the house.
8 I really regret ....*talking*......... **(talk)** to them so rudely.
9 Bill stopped ....*to drink*......... **(drink)** a glass of water and then went back to work.
10 You should try ....*going*......... **(go)** out more often if you want to meet people.

4 Put the verbs in brackets into the correct infinitive form or the -ing form, as in the example.

When I was young I used to love **1)** ...*visiting*... **(visit)** my grandparents at their cottage by the sea. I couldn't **2)** ....*wait*......... **(wait)** for the school year to end. My father would **3)** ....*drive*......... **(drive)** me to the cottage, where I loved **4)** ....*staying*... **(stay)** for the whole summer. I looked forward to **5)** ....*going*......... **(go)** fishing with my grandfather. Most days we managed **6)** ....*to catch*... **(catch)** a lot of fish but we would **7)** ....*throw*......... **(throw)** them all back into the water. Then, we would **8)** ....*swim*... **(swim)** in the clear blue sea. My grandmother loved **9)** ....*cooking*......... **(cook)** for us. I remember **10)** ....*baking*... **(bake)** chocolate chip biscuits with her. They were my favourite! She always let me **11)** ....*eat*......... **(eat)** a biscuit as soon as they came out of the oven. I can still **12)** ....*taste*... **(taste)** them now, melting in my mouth! I'll never forget **13)** ....*spending*... **(spend)** those wonderful summers with my grandparents. I will always **14)** ....*keep*...... **(keep)** the memory of them close to my heart.

5 Put the verbs in brackets into the correct infinitive form or the -ing form, as in the example.

1 A: Mum, can you **1)** ...*help*... (**help**) me with my homework? I've tried **2)** ...*to read* (**read**) the chapter by myself but it's too difficult for me **3)** ...*to understand*... (**understand**).

B: Alright, I'll **4)** ...*help*... (**help**) you in a minute.

2 A: What do you want **1)** ...*to do*... (**do**) tonight?

B: How about **2)** ...*seeing*... (**see**) a film?

A: I hate **3)** ...*going*... (**go**) to the cinema. What about **4)** ...*staying*... (**stay**) at home and **5)** ...*ordering*... (**order**) Chinese food?

B: Yeah, that sounds nice!

3 It's no use **1)** ...*talking*... (**talk**) to Rick. He's a stubborn man who refuses **2)** ...*to change*... (**change**) his mind.

4 A: Bob and Laura have decided **1)** ...*to get*... (**get**) married!

B: How wonderful!

A: Yes, it is! I was glad **2)** ...*to hear*... (**hear**) the news. I think they make a great couple.

5 Nancy is a very ambitious girl. She taught herself **1)** ...*to speak*... (**speak**) three foreign languages, and managed **2)** ...*to start*... (**start**) her own business abroad.

6 Sue was very artistic when she was young. She would **1)** ...*draw*... (**draw**) whatever was in front of her. She could also **2)** ...*make*... (**make**) jewellery. Today, she enjoys **3)** ...*teaching*... (**teach**) art to students at Warren High School. In her free time, she loves **4)** ...*painting*... (**paint**) and **5)** ...*writing*... (**write**) poetry.

6 Complete the dialogue below between a sales assistant and a customer, using the correct infinitive or -ing form.

A: Good afternoon. May I **1)** ...*help*... (**help**) you?

B: Yes, please. I'd like **2)** ...*to buy*... (**buy**) an outfit for a formal dance.

A: Of course. Now, what exactly would you like **3)** ...*to wear*... (**wear**)? A dress, a skirt and blouse or a suit?

B: Ah, I don't know.

A: Alright then. What colour are you thinking of **4)** ...*wearing*... (**wear**)?

B: I'm not sure.

A: Okay. Let's see. I think a red dress would **5)** ...*suit*... (**suit**) you ... No? Well, how about a white blouse and a black skirt ...? Not that either. Alright. A blue suit ...?

B: No, not blue. I can't stand even **6)** ...*looking*... (**look**) at that colour!

A: I see. How much money are you willing **7)** ...*to spend*... (**spend**)?

B: I want **8)** ...*to pay*... (**pay**) about £100.

A: Hmm. Perhaps you might **9)** ...*like*... (**like**) this green ballgown?

B: Yes, that's lovely. Where can I go **10)** ...*to try*... (**try**) it on?

A: The fitting room is just there, madam. I'll be right here if you need me.

7 Use the correct infinitive or -ing form of the verbs below to fill in the gaps, as in the example.

buy, brush, invite, put, see, sign, listen, tell, eat, set, drive, play

1 Steven went to the shop ...*to buy*... some stamps.

2 You must ...*brush*... your teeth at least twice a day if you want them to be healthy.

3 I'm really looking forward to ...*seeing*... the performance tonight.

4 "Oh, dear. I forgot ...*to set*... the burglar alarm before I left the house!" she said.

5 Carl really hates ...*listening*... to rap music.

6 "Excuse me. Could you please ...*tell*... me the time?" he asked.

7 Kay and Alex enjoy ...*driving*... through the countryside on Sundays.

8 "Did you remember ...*to put*... the clothes in the washing machine?" she asked.

9 Rob asked if he could ...*play*... in the park that afternoon.

10 Tom loves ...*eating*... spicy food.

11 Stacy regrets not ...*inviting*... them to her party.

12 He agreed ...*to sign*... the contract.

Revision: Units 1 - 15

Multiple Choice

8 Choose the correct item.

1 We .... the cinema when it started to snow.
A are leaving   **B** were leaving   C was leaving

2 Unless you .... some money, you won't be able to go on the trip.
A saves   B saved   **C** save

3 First she fed the cat, then she .... down at the table and read the newspaper.
A sits   **B** sat   C was sitting

4 They're the people .... live above the jewellery shop.
A who's   **B** who   C whose

5 The bags were .... heavy that I couldn't carry them.
A so   B such   C that

6 She .... her leg so she couldn't go on the skiing holiday.
A breaks   **B** had broken
C had been breaking

7 Our house .... by my father.
A build   **B** was built   C is built

8 I wish I .... my favourite bracelet.
A lost   **B** hadn't lost   C was losing

Key Word Transformation

9 Complete each sentence with two to five words, including the word in bold.

1 It was difficult for her to learn Algebra.
difficulty She .... ~~had difficulty~~ .... ~~learning~~ Algebra.

2 He was extremely nervous, yet he still gave an excellent speech.
being Despite ~~being nervous~~ .... he still gave an excellent speech.

3 "Could you go to the shop for me?" she asked.
mind "Would ~~you mind going~~ .... the shop for me?" she asked.

4 "Let's have a barbecue", Paul said.
suggested Paul ~~had suggested~~ .... ~~having~~ .... barbecue.

5 "I work in an office", Nancy said to me.
told Nancy .... ~~told~~ .... in an office.

6 The scarf was so lovely that I bought it.
such It was ~~such a lovely scarf~~ .... I bought it.

7 They have never been on an aeroplane before.
first It's the ~~first time~~ .... ~~they have been~~ .... on an aeroplane.

8 If you don't water the plants regularly, they will die.
unless The plants ~~will die if~~ .... ~~you don't water~~ .... them regularly.

Error Correction

10 Cross out the unnecessary word.

1 You should ~~to~~ leave before it gets dark.
2 The house needs be redecorating.
3 By the time they will return, I'll have finished.
4 This is my friend whose mother she is a professor.
5 If they will come early, we'll go to the theatre.

Word Formation

We can form nouns from verbs by adding these suffixes.

-al propose - proposal	**-ment** agree - agreement
-ance assist - assistance	**-sion** decide - decision
-ation relax - relaxation	(verbs ending in -d/-t sound)
-ence differ - difference	
-ion revise - revision	**-tion** describe - description

11 Fill in the gaps with the correct words derived from the words in bold.

1 Many people look forward to their .... after years of working hard.   **RETIRE**

2 Emily has a very good ~~imagination~~ ...., so she's good at writing stories.   **IMAGINE**

3 John has a ~~preference~~ .... for sweet foods, but he doesn't eat them too often.   **PREFER**

4 Tania has an amazing ~~collection~~ .... of stamps from all over the world.   **COLLECT**

5 The .... of his article in the newspaper made Peter feel very proud.   **INCLUDE**

6 A special ~~appearance~~ .... by a famous actor will be made at the club tonight.   **APPEAR**

7 The horse's ~~refusal~~ .... to jump the last fence meant that it lost the race.   **REFUSE**

8 The doctor gave me a ~~prescribe~~ .... for some tablets.   **PRESCRIBE**

Question Tags

- **Question Tags** are short questions at the end of affirmative or negative statements. We use them to ask for confirmation or agreement.
- **Question tags** are formed with an auxiliary or modal verb and an appropriate personal pronoun. If there is an auxiliary verb in the statement, the same auxiliary is used to form the question tag. Otherwise, we use **do/does** (present simple) or **did** (past simple).
  *You **can** see the stage, **can't** you?*
  *She **drives** a BMW, **doesn't** she?*
  *He **went** to Brazil, **didn't** he?*
- After affirmative statements we use a negative question tag.
  *She **is** a teacher, **isn't** she?*
- After negative statements we use a positive question tag.
  *You **haven't** fed the dog yet, **have** you?*
- When the sentence contains words such as: **never**, **hardly**, **rarely**, etc. the question tag is positive.
  *They **rarely** watch TV, **do they**?*
- The question tags of some verbs and expressions are formed differently.
  Study the examples below:
  I am ➡ aren't I? *I am clever, **aren't I**?*
  Imperative ➡ will/won't you?
  ***Be** quiet, **will/won't you**?*
  Don't ➡ will you? ***Don't yell** at me, **will you**?*
  Let's ➡ shall we? ***Let's** order a pizza, **shall we**?*
  I have (got) ➡ haven't I? (= possess)
  *He **has got** a sleeping bag, **hasn't he**?*
  I have ➡ don't I? (other meanings)
  *She **had** breakfast, **didn't she**?*
  There is/are ➡ isn't/aren't there?
  *There **is** a book on the table, **isn't there**?*
  This/That is ➡ isn't it?
  ***That is** Tom's house, **isn't it**?*

Intonation

- When we are **sure** of the answer and expect agreement, the voice goes **down** in the question tag.
  ↘
  *It's a horrible day, **isn't it**?*
- When we **aren't sure** of the answer and want to check information, the voice goes **up** in the question tag. ↗
  *The play is at eight o'clock, **isn't it**?*

Reflexive Pronouns

Singular		Plural	
I ➡ myself		we ➡ ourselves	
you ➡ yourself		you ➡ yourselves	
he ➡ himself		they ➡ themselves	
she ➡ herself			
it ➡ itself			

We use **reflexive pronouns**:
- with verbs such as **behave**, **burn**, **cut**, **enjoy**, **hurt**, **introduce**, **kill**, **look at**, **teach**, etc. or with prepositions when the subject and the object of the verb are the same.

  Lesley   has cut   **herself.**
  ↓   ↓
  (subject)   **(object)**

- with the preposition **by** when we mean **alone** (= **without company**, **on one's own**) or **without help**.
  *Helen mended the fence **by herself**. (= Nobody helped Helen mend the fence.)*
- in the following expressions: **enjoy yourself** (= have a good time), **behave yourself** (= be good), **help yourself** (= you are welcome to take something if you want).
  ***Behave yourself** at the party.*
- to emphasise the subject or the object of a sentence.
  *I painted the entire house **myself**. (= I painted the house, nobody did it for me.)*

Note:
- We do not use **reflexive pronouns** with the verbs **concentrate, feel, meet** and **relax.**
  You need to relax.
  (**NOT**: You need to relax ~~yourself~~.)
- The verbs **dress, wash** and **shave** are not normally followed by a reflexive pronoun. However, we can use a reflexive pronoun with these verbs when we want to show that someone did something with a lot of effort.
  *First I **shaved** and then I **dressed**.*
  *Although Steve is only two years old, he can **wash himself**.*

But: we always say **dry myself**.
  *I **dried myself** with a towel when I got out of the pool.*

Question Tags

1 **Underline the correct answer, as in the example.**

1 You haven't seen my keys anywhere, **haven't you/have you**?

2 You won't forget to send me a postcard, **won't you/will you**?

3 John didn't leave the shopping in the car, **did he/didn't he**?

4 You will be home early tonight, **will you/won't you**?

5 Jane is a lovely girl, **isn't she/is she**?

6 Sam went to the park today, **did he/didn't he**?

7 The Crisps haven't got any children, **haven't they/have they**?

8 Dad is sleeping, **is he/isn't he**?

9 Let's go to the circus, **shall we/will we**?

10 You've got a CD player, **have you/haven't you**?

2 **Fill in the question tags, as in the example.**

1 This is a lovely dress, ...*isn't it*........... ?
2 Let's go for a walk, ...shall........ ?
3 Jenny has got a canary, ...hasn't she..... ?
4 You don't like watching TV, ...do you....... ?
5 Don't be long, ...will you....... ?
6 This is Tommy's bicycle, ...isn't it....... ?
7 He exercises every day, ...doesn't he...... ?
8 Martha hasn't got a car, ...has she..... ?
9 I'm not late, ...am I........ ?
10 We aren't invited to their wedding, ...are we........ ?

3 **Fill in the correct question tags and short answers, as in the example.**

1 A: Frank has got a brother, ...*hasn't he*... ?
   B: Yes, ...*he has*... .

2 A: Susan isn't a mechanic, ...is she......... ?
   B: No, ...
3 A: Lynn and Ian don't live here, ...do they...... ?
   B: No, ...
4 A: You've been to Greece, ...haven't you........
   B: Yes, ...
5 A: They rarely go to the beach, ...do they..... ?
   B: No, ...they don't... .
6 A: This is Doug's briefcase, ...isn't it........ ?
   B: Yes, ...
7 A: He's not ill, ...is he........ ?
   B: No, ...he isn't...... .
8 A: There is a dog in the garden, ...isn't there...... ?
   B: Yes, ...
9 A: They got married, ...didn't they..... ?
   B: Yes, ...they did...... .
10 A: You aren't old enough to drive, ...are you...... ?
    B: No, ...I amn't.... .
11 A: That is Bill's car, ...isn't it........ ?
    B: Yes, ...
12 A: You will remember to call me, ...won't you...... ?
    B: Yes, ...I will...... .

4 **Fill in the question tags, as in the example, then read the sentences with the correct intonation.**

		sure	not sure
1	You walk to school, ...*don't you*... ?	✓	
2	That man is very handsome, ...isn't he........ ?	✓	
3	She graduated last year, ...didn't she........ ?		✓
4	They're coming, ...aren't they......?		✓
5	You've posted the letters, ...haven't you........ ?	✓	
6	He lives in Rome, ...doesn't he......?		✓
7	Your mother is a teacher, ...isn't she........ ?	✓	
8	He'll drive me to the bank, ...won't he........ ?	✓	
9	You don't like fish, ...do you......?		✓
10	That's Pete's dog, ...isn't it......?	✓	

5 **Fill in the gaps with the correct question tag, as in the example.**

A: Natalie's coming home this weekend, **1)** *...isn't she...* ?
B: Yes, I can't wait. You haven't seen her in ages, **2)** ...*have you*...?
A: No, the last time I saw her was at Christmas.
B: She has called you since then, **3)** ...*hasn't she*...?
A: Oh, yes. We speak to each other every week.
B: Well, you know her parents are having a party on Saturday, **4)** ...*don't you*...? Everybody's going. You and Dave will be there, **5)** ...*won't you*...?
A: Definitely! Johnny's playing the music, **6)** ...*isn't he*...?
B: I'm not sure. But if he is, it's going to be a great party.

Reflexive Pronouns

6 **Fill in the appropriate reflexive pronoun, as in the example.**

1 A: Shall I iron your shirt?
   B: No, that's alright. I'll iron it *...myself...* .
2 A: So, how was the show last night?
   B: Fantastic! We really enjoyed ...*ourselves*... .
3 A: Please, help ...*yourself*... to more tea.
   B: Thank you.
4 A: Did the Whites have their wedding cake made by the local bakery?
   B: No, they made it ...*themselves*... .
5 A: Did you buy those books for Don?
   B: No, I bought them for ...*myself*... .
6 A: Why is Sandra wearing a bandage on her finger?
   B: She cut ...*myself*... on a piece of broken glass.
7 A: Your daughter is very clever, isn't she?
   B: Yes, she taught ...*herself*... to speak Japanese.
8 A: Shall I turn off the air-conditioning?
   B: No, it will turn ...*itself*... off when the air is cooler.

9 A: Did you take your car to the garage?
   B: No, I managed to fix it ...*myself*... .
10 A: Can you make me a sandwich, please?
   B: No, make it ...*yourself*... .

7 **Look at the pictures and then fill in the gaps with the correct reflexive pronoun, as in the example.**

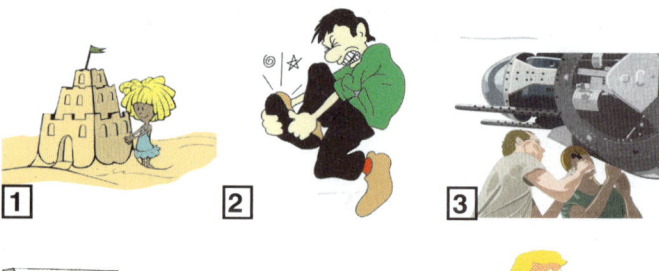

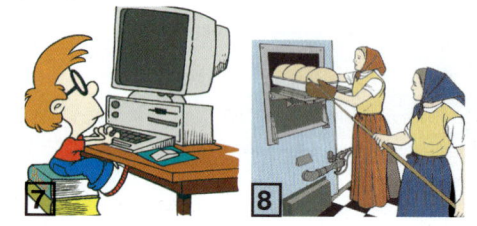

1 The little girl built a sandcastle by .....*herself*..... .
2 He has hurt ...*himself*... .
3 They fixed the engine ...*themselves*... .
4 She is sitting by ...*herself*... .
5 He is building his house by ...*himself*... .
6 She bought a bicycle for ...*them*... .
7 He taught ...*himself*... how to use a computer.
8 They baked the bread ...*themselves*... .

8 **Complete the following sentences using a word from the list below and a reflexive pronoun.**

locked, design, switches, hurt,
poured, cut, made, serve

1 This is a self-service restaurant. You have to ...*serve yourself*... .
2 We were hungry so we ...*made*... ...*ourselves*... some sandwiches.
3 I ...*cut myself*... while I was slicing some bread.
4 Did Deborah ...*design*... her wedding dress ...*herself*...?
5 After a while, he got up and ...*poured*... ...*himself*... a glass of water.

6 The kettle .... off when the water has boiled.

7 The clown pretended he had .... and everyone roared with laughter.

8 They .... out of the house.

Revision: Units 1 - 16

Multiple Choice

9 Choose the correct item.

1 That lasagne was .... delicious that I'm definitely going to make it again.
   A much   **B** so   **C** such

2 How long has Mum .... ?
   A been sleeping   **B** was sleeping   **C** is sleeping

3 The family .... live down the street are from Argentina.
   A who   **B** whom   **C** which

4 My father .... in the garden every weekend.
   A was working   **B** is working   **C** works

5 "Why did she .... everybody about the party?" he asked.
   A advise   **B** tell   **C** say

6 .... he's got a car, he walks everywhere.
   A However   **B** Although   **C** But

7 Our newspaper .... every day by our neighbour's son.
   A delivers   **B** is delivered   **C** delivered

8 It is believed that she .... the competition.
   A will win   **B** wins   **C** haven't won

9 I love feeding the ducks in .... Hyde Park.
   A a   **B** the   **C** —

10 We have been best friends .... twenty-five years.
   A just   **B** since   **C** for

11 She used .... ballet lessons when she was young.
   A to take   **B** to taking   **C** taking

12 Alison refused .... to her brother.
   A talk   **B** to talk   **C** talking

Key Word Transformation

10 Complete each sentence with two to five words, including the word in bold.

1 It was such a bad storm that I was afraid to drive the car.
   so   The storm ....
   .... I was afraid to drive the car.

2 The company he works for imports Italian shoes.
   which   The company ....
   .... imports Italian shoes.

3 They have never been to the ballet before.
   first   It's the ....
   .... to the ballet.

4 She hasn't finished her homework yet.
   still   She ....
   .... homework.

5 When did you get married?
   ago   How long ....
   .... married?

6 Pete turned off his computer and left the office.
   after   Pete left the office...............................
   .... his computer.

7 "I don't know what to have for dinner," said Arthur.
   didn't   Arthur said that.................................
   .... to have for dinner.

8 It's forbidden to feed the animals at the zoo.
   mustn't You ....
   .... at the zoo.

9 Swans are more beautiful than ducks.
   not   Ducks ....
   .... swans.

Word Formation

11 Fill in the gaps with the correct words derived from the words in bold.

My great-grandmother, Frances Thompson, was a very **1)** .... woman. **TALENT**
She was a **2)** .... but she also **TEACH** loved to paint and draw things. For years she tried to become a **3)** .... **SUCCESS** artist, but she never became **4)** .... **FAME** .... However, she enjoyed teaching a lot, so she wasn't **5)** .... **HAPPY** She taught in a primary school for forty years and when she retired she joined a club in order to meet more people and managed to make friends **6)** .... **EASY** .... I still have some of the paintings which she gave to me years ago.

Plurals

Regular Plurals			
packet ➡ packets			
witch ➡ witches			
potato ➡ potatoes		photo ➡ photos	
lady ➡ ladies	**BUT**	boy ➡ boys	
calf ➡ calves		roof ➡ roofs	

Irregular Plurals			
man ➡ **men**		mouse ➡ **mice**	
woman ➡ **women**		sheep ➡ **sheep**	
child ➡ **children**		ox ➡ **oxen**	
foot ➡ **feet**		fish ➡ **fish**	
tooth ➡ **teeth**		louse ➡ **lice**	

- Some nouns are always plural and take a plural verb: **clothes**, **police**, **trousers**, **pyjamas**, **binoculars**, **scales**, **scissors**, **spectacles**, **outskirts**, **savings**, **stairs**, **surroundings**, etc.
- Some nouns of Greek or Latin origin form their plurals according to the rules of Greek or Latin:
  crisis ➡ **crises**
  phenomenon ➡ **phenomena**
  datum ➡ **data**
  medium ➡ **media** etc.
- We normally add **-s** to the last word of compound nouns.
  girlfriend ➡ **girlfriends**
  washing machine ➡ **washing machines**
  BUT
  brother-in-law ➡ **brothers-in-law**
  passer-by ➡ **passers-by**

Clauses of Reason and Result

- We use **clauses of reason** to express the reason for something. They are introduced with:
- **as/since**
  She got up late as/since it was Sunday.
- **because**
  I ate a sandwich because I was hungry.
- **because of/due to + noun**
  The road was closed because of/due to bad weather.
- **because of the fact/due to the fact that**
  Because of/Due to the fact that there was bad weather, the roads were closed.

- We use **clauses of result** to express the result of something. They are introduced with:
- **so + adjective/adverb**
  The concert was so exciting (that) everyone was dancing.
- **such a/an + adjective + singular countable noun**
  She is such an intelligent woman (that) everybody admires her.
- **such + adjective + plural/uncountable noun**
  They were such difficult questions (that) nobody could answer them.
  It was such delicious food (that) we all had second helpings.

Too/Enough

- **Too + adjective/adverb** has a negative meaning. We use it to show that something is more than enough, necessary or wanted.
  She's too old to play with dolls.
- **Adjective/Adverb + enough** has a positive meaning. We use it to show that there is as much of something as is wanted or needed.
  She's strong enough to carry the boxes.

All/Both/Neither/None

- **All** refers to more than two people, things or groups. It has a positive meaning and it takes a plural verb.
  All the children wore costumes.
  All of them were young.
  All of their costumes were colourful.
- **Both** refers to two people, things or groups. It has a positive meaning and it takes a plural verb.
  Both of my brothers play basketball.
- **Neither** refers to two people, things or groups. It has a negative meaning. **Neither of + plural noun phrase** takes either a singular or plural verb in the affirmative.
  Neither of the men is/are from Tokyo.
- **None of** refers to more than two people, things or groups. It has a negative meaning, and it takes either a singular or a plural verb in the affirmative.
  None of these dresses suits/suit me.

Plurals

1 **Write the plural of the following nouns, as in the example.**

1 mother-in-law
   ...mothers-in-law...
2 pouch ....
3 river ....
4 comb ....
5 swimming pool
   ....

6 louse ....
7 father ....
8 keyhole ....
9 foot ....
10 teacup ....
11 notebook ....
12 glass ....

2 **Underline the correct word, as in the example.**

1 A: How many **apple**/**apples** are there in the bowl?
   B: Just three.
2 A: Do you like my new **haircuts**/**haircut**?
   B: Oh, yes. It's lovely.
3 A: Would you like a **glass**/**glasses** of water?
   B: No, thanks.
4 A: Do you know those **boy**/**boys** over there?
   B: Yes, they're my brother's friends.
5 A: Mary found two **mice**/**mouse** in her attic yesterday.
   B: Oh, how horrible!
6 A: Did you know that Mr Howard's **wife**/**wives** is a famous violinist?
   B: No, I had no idea.
7 A: Could you pass me that **dictionary**/**dictionaries**, please?
   B: Yes, certainly.
8 A: Connie bought two lovely antique **teapots**/**teapot** at the fair today.
   B: That's nice.

Clauses of Reason and Result

3 **Complete each sentence with two to five words, including the word in bold.**

1 Sandra took an umbrella with her because it was raining.
   since Sandra took an umbrella with her .... raining.
2 He didn't pass his exam, so he was upset.
   due He was upset .... he didn't pass his exam.
3 She didn't have any tomatoes, so she didn't make a salad.
   as She didn't make a salad .... any tomatoes.

4 There was a lot of traffic, so they were late for work.
   because They were late for work................... .... of traffic.
5 He was fired because he was very lazy.
   due He was fired .... he was lazy.

4 **Fill in the gaps with *so, such* or *such a (an)*, as in the example.**

1 A: I love this restaurant.
   B: So do I! The food is ...*so*... delicious that I come here every Friday.
2 A: Are you going to the concert tonight?
   B: I don't think so. I have .... bad headache that I think I'll stay at home.
3 A: How was Pete's party on Friday?
   B: Fantastic! He played .... great music that we danced all night long.
4 A: Did you go to the park yesterday?
   B: No, it was .... windy that we stayed in instead.
5 A: Why isn't Paula coming with us this weekend?
   B: Well, she spent .... lot of money redecorating her flat that she can't afford to go anywhere for a while.
6 A: Is there any curry left?
   B: No, sorry. It was .... tasty that we ate it all.

Too/Enough

5 **Complete the sentences with *too* or *enough* and the adjectives in brackets, as in the example.**

1 A: Does your son stay at home alone?
   B: No, he's ...*too young*... to stay at home alone. **(young)**

2 A: Let's play cards.

B: No, I'm .... to play cards. **(tired)**

3 A: Can you lift that suitcase?

B: I don't think so. I'm not .... **(strong)**
.... to lift it.

4 A: Did you go to the beach yesterday?

B: No, it was .... **(cloudy)**
to go to the beach.

5 A: So, did you join the basketball team?

B: No, I'm not .... to join. **(tall)**

6 A: Did you see Don last night?

B: No, he was .... **(busy)**
to see me.

6 **Match Column A to Column B.**

A	B
1 Paul and David are too young	**A** for Billy to buy with his savings.
2 It isn't warm enough today	**B** to catch the express train to London this morning.
3 Lizzie didn't get up early enough	**C** to win the race at school last Monday.
4 The old wooden wardrobe was too heavy	**D** to phone Jim. You can phone him in the morning.
5 Jane got to the bank too late	**E** to go on holiday abroad by themselves.
6 This car is old, but it's cheap enough	**F** to speak to the manager about a loan.
7 Linda isn't tall enough	**G** to be a model, although she would like to be one.
8 It's eleven o'clock. It's too late	**H** to go for a picnic on the beach.
9 Edward ran too slowly	**I** for them to lift, so they asked Tom to help them.

7 **Rewrite the following sentences using *too,* as in the example.**

1 The soup was so salty that I couldn't eat it.

...The soup was too salty for me to eat....

2 The road was so slippery that she couldn't drive.

....
....

3 The water is so cold that they can't swim in it.

....
....

4 It is so dark that I can't see.

....
....

5 The earrings were so expensive that she couldn't buy them.

....
....

6 These potatoes are so hot that I can't eat them.

....
....

7 The steak was so tough that he couldn't cut it.

....
....

8 The article was so difficult that they couldn't understand it.

....
....

All/Both/Neither/None

8 **Fill in the gaps with *all, both, neither* or *none,* as in the example.**

1 ...*Both*... wolves and cats are mammals; .... of them are birds.

2 .... of the animals have horns.

3 .... cats and birds can be domesticated.

4 .... of the animals have tails.

5 .... cats and wolves are carnivores;
.... of them are vegetarians.

6 .... of the animals have claws.

7 .... wolves and cats have noses;
.... of them have beaks.

Revision: Units 1 - 17

Multiple Choice

9 **Choose the correct item.**

1 I would love .... to the rock festival.

A go   **B** to going   **C** to go

2 Linda's coming for dinner, ... ?
  A isn't she   B hasn't she   C wasn't she

3 Bill fixed the fridge by ....
  A himself   B him   C his

4 If I had a car, I .... everywhere.
  A am driving   B will drive   C would drive

5 Being a taxi driver is an interesting job. ...., it can be very tiring.
  A What is more   B However   C Also

6 The Mayor .... to be elected again this year.
  A expect   B will expect   C is expected

7 My mother works .... a librarian at my school.
  A such   B as   C like

8 He warned us not .... the dog.
  A stroke   B stroking   C to stroke

9 If I ...., I would have babysat for you.
  A had known   B did know   C knew

10 She .... graduated by the time you see her again.
  A will have   B will be   C would have

Key Word Transformation

10 **Complete each sentence with two to five words, including the word in bold.**

1 The house she lives in used to be owned by a famous writer.
  which   The house ....
  .... used
  to be owned by a famous writer.

2 The bed was so uncomfortable that I couldn't sleep in it.
  too   The bed ....
  .... to sleep in.

3 If you don't finish your homework, you can't go to the party.
  unless   You can't go to the party ....
  .... homework.

4 They will announce the President's plans next week.
  be   The President's plans ....
  .... week.

5 "Could you get me my slippers, please?" said Helen.
  mind   "Would ....
  .... slippers, please?" said Helen.

6 "Let's meet at the train station," Jane said.
  suggested   Jane ....
  .... train station.

7 I think you should eat more fruit.
  were   If ....
  .... eat more fruit.

8 The Beatles sang *Yellow Submarine*.
  by   *Yellow Submarine* ....
  .... The Beatles.

9 "You broke the window," he said to Colin.
  accused   He ....
  .... the window.

10 "Have you read any good books lately?" she asked Bob.
  if   She asked Bob.............................
  .... good books lately.

11 I feel really awful because I didn't call her back.
  wish   I ....
  .... her back.

12 "What did you do this afternoon?" Kelly asked Harry.
  done   Kelly asked Harry ....
  .... afternoon.

Word Formation

11 **Fill in the gaps with the correct words derived from the words in bold.**

Oysters are shellfish which are 1) .... **USUAL** found on the 2) .... bottoms **ROCK** of seas and oceans. Oysters can be eaten, and many people find them extremely 3) .... However, some **TASTE** types of oyster cannot be eaten, but they produce 4) .... pearls instead. **BEAUTY** In some places, 5) .... go to **DIVE** the bottom of the ocean to collect oysters and look inside them for pearls. Jewellery made of pearls is very 6) .... **VALUE** and is expensive to buy.

Clauses of Purpose

We use **clauses of purpose** to express the purpose of an action, i.e. why someone does something. They are introduced with:

- **to -infinitive:**
  *I'm going to the shop **to get** a newspaper.*
- **in order to (formal):**
  *She went to the bank **in order to** apply for a loan.*
  In negative sentences we use **in order not to.**
  *He set the alarm clock **in order not to** wake up late.* (**NOT:** *He set the alarm clock ~~not to~~ wake up late.*)
- **so that + can/will (present or future reference).** We use **can** and **will** when the verb in the main clause is in a present or future tense.
  *She studies every day **so that** she **can** pass her exams.*
- **so that + could/would (past reference).** We use **could** and **would** when the main verb is in a past tense.
  *They booked their tickets in advance **so that** they **wouldn't** have to queue.*

Note: **In order that** has the same meaning as **so that**, but it is not used very often because it is formal.
*She studies every day **in order that** she **can** pass her exams.*

---

1 Underline the correct word(s), as in the example.

1 She went to the chemists **so that/to** get some cough syrup.
2 He bought a video **in order to/so that** record his favourite programmes.
3 They left the house early **so that/to** they would arrive on time.
4 He goes to the gym every day **in order to/so that** he can lose some weight.
5 She went to Madrid **to/so that** learn Spanish.
6 They sold their house **so that/to** they could buy a bungalow.
7 They arrived early **in order not to/not to** miss the firework display.
8 She went to the countryside **so that/to** take a walk in the fresh air.
9 I ordered a Chinese takeaway **in order to/so that** I wouldn't have to cook.

2 Join the following sentences using *to* as in the example.

1 We stopped using plastic bags. We wanted to protect the environment.
   ...*We stopped using plastic bags to protect the environment.*...
2 Sandra takes the bus to work. She wants to help reduce traffic pollution.
   ....
   ....

3 My class adopted an endangered animal. We wanted to save it from extinction.
   ....
   ....
4 Sandra went to the greengrocer's. She wanted to buy some vegetables.
   ....
   ....
5 We should all volunteer to patrol our forests. We want to protect them from fires.
   ....
   ....
6 The government has introduced stricter traffic laws. They want to reduce road accidents.
   ....
   ....
7 Mike offered me some flowers. He wanted to apologise for his behaviour.
   ....
   ....
8 She spent the summer in Rome. She wanted to improve her Italian.
   ....
   ....
9 Bob called his brother. He wanted to tell him about his new job.
   ....
   ....

3 You are going on a camping trip to the mountains and you are talking to a friend about what you should take with you. First, match Column A to Column B, then ask and answer questions, as in the example.

A

1 matches
2 penknife
3 sleeping bag
4 tent
5 radio
6 torch
7 insect repellent
8 compass

B

a to sleep in
b to stay in
c to see in the dark
d to avoid being bitten by mosquitoes
e to light a fire
f to find your way
g to open canned food
h to listen to the weather forecast

(1=e) A: *Should I take matches with me?*
B: *Yes. Take matches* **so that you can/in order to** *light a fire.*

4 Join the sentences using the word(s) in brackets, as in the example.

1 I've enrolled on an art course. I want to learn how to draw. **(to)**
I've enrolled on an art course to learn how to draw.

2 She circled the day on her calendar. She didn't want to miss the appointment. **(so that)**
....

3 She bought a phone card from the shop. She wanted to make some phone calls. **(in order to)**
....

4 He wrote down the address. He didn't want to forget it. **(in order not to)**
....

5 Pierre is taking gourmet cookery classes. He wants to be a chef. **(so that)**
....

6 He is learning karate. He wants to be able to defend himself. **(so that)**
....

7 The nurse came into the waiting room. She wanted to call the next patient. **(to)**
....

8 She went to bed at ten o'clock. She didn't want to wake up late the next morning. **(in order not to)**
....

9 Ann worked hard. She wanted to finish her report on time. **(so that)**
....

10 We should set up more wildlife parks. We must protect animals from hunters. **(in order to)**
....

11 Sue called her best friend. She wanted to tell her the great news. **(to)**
....

12 They put the gifts under the Christmas tree. They wanted the children to see them in the morning. **(so that)**
....

13 They are throwing a big party. They want to celebrate their 10th wedding anniversary. **(in order to)**
....

14 He bought a second-hand car. He didn't want to spend too much money. **(in order not to)**
....

5 Complete each sentence with two to five words, including the word in bold.

1 We should recycle paper. We want to protect the forests.

that ...We should recycle paper ...*so that we can protect*... the forests.

2 She took extra money with her. She wanted to buy some souvenirs.

order She took extra money with her ....
.... some souvenirs.

3 I had a glass of water before I went to bed. I didn't want to be thirsty during the night.

that I had a glass of water before I went to bed ....
.... be thirsty during the night.

4 Helen went to the travel agent's. She wanted to get some information about Canada.

order Helen went to the travel agent's ....
....
information about Canada.

5 They arrived at the airport three hours early. They didn't want to miss their flight.

not They arrived at the airport three hours early ....
.... their flight.

6 Dave called the police station. He wanted to report a break-in at his flat.

order Dave called the police station ....
....
.... a break-in at his flat.

7 He practises playing the piano every day. He wants to pass his music exam.

that He practises playing the piano every day .... his music exam.

8 Susan called Vicky. She wanted to ask her advice about something.

to Susan called Vicky ....
.... about something.

9 He entered the room quietly. He didn't want to wake up the baby.

not He entered the room quietly ....
.... up the baby.

Multiple Choice

6 Choose the correct item.

1 It was .... boring lecture that I almost fell asleep.

A such a   B so   C such

2 Kenya is a country .... is situated in east Africa.

A who's   B who   C which

3 She .... the dog a bath when the doorbell rang.

A was giving   B gave   C give

4 They have never .... to a rock concert.

A go   B gone   C been

5 Angel's been singing with the band .... eight months.

A for   B since   C still

6 I have always wanted to ride a camel across .... Sahara Desert.

A —   B the   C a

7 She always .... a lot of pepper on her food.

A has put   B put   C puts

8 Carla hopes she .... her own boutique by the time she's forty years old.

A opens   B will open
C will have opened

9 He accused me of .... his wallet.

A steal   B stealing   C have stolen

10 The new school .... by the mayor yesterday morning.

A was opened   B is opened   C opened

11 If I lived in the country, I .... my own vegetables.

A grow   B will grow   C would grow

12 We .... a wonderful time in Mexico.
   A are having   **B** have   **C** has
13 She .... to breaking the window.
   A denied   **B** admitted   **C** refused
14 .... he is a clever boy, he isn't a good student.
   A Because   **B** However   **C** Although
15 I used .... football when I was younger.
   A play   **B** to playing   **C** to play

Key Word Transformation

7 **Complete each sentence with two to five words, including the word in bold.**

1 Mario is the mechanic. He works at the local garage.
   who   Mario is ....
   .... at the local garage.
2 The trip was postponed because of the bad weather.
   due   The trip ....
   .... the bad weather.
3 The puppy is not old enough to be taken away from its mother.
   young   The puppy is ....
   .... away from its mother.
4 You'll catch cold if you don't put on your coat.
   unless   You'll catch cold ....
   .... your coat.
5 Could you drive me to the city centre?
   mind   Would ....
   .... the city centre?
6 You shouldn't spend all your money.
   were   If I ....
   .... spend all my money.
7 Who made this delicious bread?
   made   Who ....
   .... by?
8 It's not necessary to come to work on Saturday.
   needn't   You ....
   .... on Saturday.
9 "Put your toys away!" Mum said.
   me   Mum ....
   .... toys away.
10 I advise you to wear your glasses more often.
   should   You ....
   .... glasses more often.
11 It was such a long flight that they were exhausted when they reached their destination.
   so   The flight ....
   .... they
   were exhausted when they reached
   their destination.

Error Correction

8 **Cross out the unnecessary word.**

1 She often reads before to going to sleep.
2 Have you heard of the latest song by Celine Dion?
3 You needn't to call a taxi. I'll give you a lift.
4 She's the most beautiful baby I have ever had seen.
5 If you see Bill, tell to him to call me at the office.
6 Carol was be washing the dishes when the phone rang.
7 You will be in trouble unless you not tell the truth.
8 Take an umbrella before you will leave the house.

Word Formation

9 **Fill in the gaps with the correct words derived from the words in bold.**

One cold and **1)** .... night, a **STORM**
group of ghost- **2)** .... **HUNT**
went on a trip to Dark Towers, which is a
3) .... castle in a remote part **HAUNT**
of Scotland. They walked **4)** .... **SLOW**
into the **5)** .... castle and began **MYSTERY**
to look around. There were no lights, so
they used torches as they searched. The
6) .... of the castle was **SILENT**
very **7)** ...., so they stayed **FRIGHTEN**
together for safety. Suddenly, they saw a
8) .... figure on the stairs. **GHOST**
Through the **9)** .... they could **DARK**
see that it was a woman in a long dress.
She was crying **10)** .... The ghost **QUIET**
was so **11)** .... that the ghost- **SCARE**
hunters all screamed **12)** .... **LOUD**
and ran out of the castle. They never went
back again.

Countable/Uncountable Nouns

- **Countable nouns** are those that can be counted. They have singular and plural forms (*one peach, two peaches,* etc.).
- **Uncountable nouns** are those that cannot be counted (*milk, flour,* etc.). Uncountable nouns take a singular verb and are not used with a/an. These are:

  types of food (*bread, cheese,* etc.)
  liquids (*water, petrol,* etc.)
  subjects of study (*History, Chemistry,* etc.)
  languages (*English, Portuguese,* etc.)
  sports (*tennis, baseball,* etc.)
  diseases (*malaria, flu,* etc.)
  natural phenomena (*rain, fog,* etc.)
  certain nouns (*advice, dirt, education, luck, news, peace, traffic, weather, homework, music, information, seaside, shopping, trouble, work,* etc.)
  collective nouns (*furniture, money, rubbish, jewellery, luggage,* etc.)
- We can use both **uncountable nouns** and **countable nouns** after phrases of quantity such as: *a jar/bottle/piece/loaf/cup/glass/kilo/carton/bowl/ can/tin/slice/packet of,* etc.
  *She ate two **slices of bread**. I need a **kilo of tomatoes**.*

Some/Any/No

Affirmative			
Adjectives	**Pronouns**		**Adverbs**
	people	**things**	**places**
some	someone/ somebody	something	somewhere
any	anyone/ anybody	anything	anywhere

Negative			
Adjectives	**Pronouns**		**Adverbs**
	people	**things**	**places**
no/not any	no one/ not anyone nobody/ not anybody	nothing/ not anything	nowhere/ not anywhere

Interrogative			
Adjectives	**Pronouns**		**Adverbs**
	people	**things**	**places**
any	anyone/ anybody	anything	anywhere

- **Some** and **its compounds** (someone, something, etc.) are normally used in **positive sentences**. They can also be used in **questions** to make an **offer**, a **request** or when we **expect a positive answer**.
  *I bought **some** books yesterday. **(positive)***
  *Would you like **something** to drink? **(offer)***
  *Can I have **something** to eat? **(request)***

- **Any** and **its compounds** (anyone, anything, etc.) are normally used in questions and negations.
  *There aren't **any** apples left. **(negation)***
  *Is there **anything** I can make for the party? **(question)***
  They can also be used in positive sentences meaning "It doesn't matter how/what/when/where/which/who, etc."
  *You can ask **anybody** to go with you. (= it doesn't matter who)*
  Any and **its compounds** can be used after **if** in a positive sentence. *If you need **anything**, please tell me.*
  They are also used with **negative words** (hardly, never, without, seldom, rarely, etc.)
  *She **never** goes out with **anyone** from work.*
  (**NOT**: *She never goes out with ~~no one~~ from work.*)

- **No/Not any** and **their compounds** (no one/not anyone, nothing/not anything, etc.) are used in negations.
  *There is **no** milk. (= There is**n't any** milk.)*
  *There's **no one** in the house. (= There is**n't anyone** in the house.)*

Much/Many

- **Much** and **many** are normally used in questions and negations. **Much** is used with **uncountable nouns** and **many** is used with **plural countable nouns**.
  *There isn't **much coffee** in the jar.*
  *Have you got **many books**?*

- **How much** and **how many** are used in questions.
  How much + uncountable noun → amount
  How many + countable noun → number
  How much sugar do we need? Not much.
  How many people came to the party? Twenty.

Countable/Uncountable Nouns - Some/Any/No - Much/Many - (A) few/(A) little - Comparative/Superlative Form - Expressing Preference

19

A few/Few/A little/Little

- We use **few** (= not many, almost none)/**a few** (= some/not many) with plural countable nouns.
  Few people liked the performance. (= almost none)
  I've got a few oranges. (= a small number, not many)
- We use **little** (= not much, almost none)/**a little** (= some/not much) with uncountable nouns.
  There is little milk left. (= almost none)
  I'd like a little sugar in my coffee, please. (= not much)

Comparative/Superlative Form

- We use the **comparative form** + **than** to compare two people, things, places, etc.
  Rob is stronger than Tim.
- We use **the** + **superlative form** + **of/in** to compare a person, thing or place with the whole group they belong to. We use **in** when we talk about places.
  Sue is the shortest of her friends. Lisbon is the most beautiful city in Europe.

Form

- We add **-(e)r/-(e)st** to **one-syllable** and **two-syllable** adjectives to form their comparative and superlative forms.
  tall - tall**er** (than) - **the** tall**est** (of/in)
- Adjectives of three or more syllables take **more** and **most**.
  beautiful - **more** beautiful - **the most** beautiful
  Note: The comparative and superlative forms of **clever, common, cruel, friendly, gentle, narrow, pleasant, polite, shallow, simple, stupid, quiet** are formed with **-er/-est** or **more/most**.
  gentle - gentler - the gentlest Also: *gentle - **more** gentle - the **most** gentle.*

Spelling

- One-syllable adjectives ending in **-e** take **-r** in the comparative form and **-st** in the superlative form.
  nice - nicer - nicest

- Two-syllable adjectives ending in **-y** turn the **-y** into **i** and then take **-er/est**.
  funny - funnier - funniest
- Adjectives ending in a stressed vowel between two consonants double the final consonant and take **-er/-est**.
  big - bigger - biggest
  but: *strong - stronger - strongest*

Irregular forms		
Adjective	**Comparative**	**Superlative**
good	better	the best
bad	worse	the worst
much/many/ a lot of }	more	the most
little	less	the least
far	further/farther	the furthest/ farthest

Types of Comparison

- We use **as** + **adjective** + **as** to show that two people or things are similar. In negative sentences we use **not as/so ... as**.
  Betty is as tall as her mother.
  Adam isn't as/so friendly as Tom.
- We use **less** + **adjective** + **than** for two people or things. It is the opposite of **more ... than**.
  Tom's bike was less expensive than mine.

Expressing Preference

- **prefer** + **-ing form/noun** + **to** + **-ing form/noun**
  I prefer working in the garden to watching TV.
  I prefer milk to tea.
- **would prefer** + **to -inf** + **rather than** + **inf without to**
  I would prefer to read a book rather than go for a walk.
- **would rather** + **inf without to** + **than** + **inf without to**
  I would/'d rather own a house than rent one.

Countable/Uncountable Nouns

1 Fill in the gaps with *is, are, a* or *some*.

1 Physics .... my favourite subject.
2 The fog .... very thick, I can't see.
3 The weather .... nice today.
4 Where .... the milk?
5 Let me give you .... advice.
6 The traffic .... terrible in the city centre.
7 Apples .... my least favourite fruit.
8 The furniture .... in storage until the new house is ready.
9 I've got .... good news.
10 I need .... loaf of bread.

2 Fill in the gaps with an appropriate *noun + of* to indicate quantity, then make sentences, as in the example.

1 ... *a carton of...* orange juice
2 .... water
3 .... popcorn
4 .... pizza
5 .... bread
6 .... coffee
7 .... milk
8 .... soda
9 .... cake
10 .... mustard

I'd like a carton of orange juice, please.

Some/Any/No

3 Fill in the gaps with *some*, *any*, *no* or one of their compounds, as in the example.

1 A: How was your skiing weekend?
 B: Terrible! There was hardly ...*any*... snow on the mountains.
2 A: There are .... really fascinating exhibits at the new museum.
 B: Really! I must go.

3 A: Hurry up! There's ...*no*... time to waste. The bus will be here soon.
 B: I'm nearly ready.
4 A: Did you visit Henry today?
 B: No. When I called his house ...*no*... answered the phone.
5 A: Do you want to go to the cinema tonight?
 B: No, thanks. There's .... I want to see.
6 A: Can I get you ...*anything*... from the shop?
 B: Just a bag of crisps, thanks.
7 A: I bought ...*some*... great books from the book fair this afternoon.
 B: Really! Let me see.
8 A: I've always wanted to go ...*somewhere*... exotic for my holidays.
 B: Why don't you go to Tahiti, then?

4 Underline the correct word, as in the example.

1 **Somebody**/**Anybody** broke into our house last night.
2 I had **any**/**no** time to go to the post office today.
3 Are you going **nowhere**/**anywhere** nice for your holidays?
4 There was **anyone**/**no one** left at the party by two o'clock.
5 **Nobody**/**Somebody** is allowed to park in front of this building.
6 Have I done **something**/**nothing** to offend you?
7 If **no one**/**anyone** is looking for me, tell them I've gone home.
8 It will take you **any**/**some** time to get used to such a hot climate.

Much/Many

5 Fill in the gaps with *How many* or *How much*, as in the example.

1 ...*How much*... yogurt?
2 .... books?
3 .... potatoes?
4 .... soap?
5 .... onions?
6 .... pens?
7 .... glue?
8 .... cheese?
9 .... keys?
10 .... apples?
11 .... coffee?
12 .... pepper?
13 .... cabbage?
14 .... biscuits?
15 .... water?
16 .... paper?
17 .... cherries?
18 .... milk?
19 .... mustard?
20 .... popcorn?

6 Fill in the dialogue below with *much, many, how much* or *how many*, as in the example.

A: Let's make lasagne for the dinner party tomorrow.
B: Great idea! **1)** ...*How much*... minced meat do we need?
A: Not **2)** .... Half a kilo will do.
B: OK. **3)** .... tomatoes?
A: About three big ones.
B: **4)** .... cheese should I buy?
A: Get about half a kilo of mozarella.
B: Right. Now, **5)** ....packets of lasagne will we need?
A: One packet will be enough.
B: What about onions? We haven't got **6)** .... left.
A: We only need two. Is there any milk in the fridge?
B: Well, there is some but not **7)** ....
A: You'd better buy a carton then. And get some flour as well.
B: **8)** .... flour shall I buy?
A: A small packet will be enough.
B: OK. I'll be back in about an hour.

A few/A little

7 Fill in the gaps with *a few* or *a little*, as in the example.

1 A: What would you like in your coffee?
   B: Just ...*a little*... sugar, please.
2 A: Are you going to buy that jacket you saw last week?
   B: No. I've only got .... money left so I can't afford it.
3 A: Could I have .... more ice cubes in my drink, please?
   B: Certainly.
4 A: There are still .... tickets left for the concert on Friday night.
   B: Great. I'll go and buy one now.
5 A: Only .... people know that Karen used to be a famous ballet dancer.
   B: Really? I had no idea.

6 A: This curry isn't spicy.
   B: Well, why don't you add .... curry powder to it?

8 Ask and answer questions using the prompts below, as in the example.

1 oranges

2 meat

3 prawns

4 tomato juice

5 bread

6 olives

7 croissants

8 green peppers

9 coffee

1 A: *Did you buy many oranges?*
   B: *No, just a few.*
2 A: *Did you buy much meat?*
   B: *No, just a little.*

Comparative/Superlative Forms

9 Fill in the gaps with *than, the, of* or *in*, as in the example.

1 The Eiffel Tower is one of ...*the*... most famous monuments ...*in*... the world.
2 John's new house is bigger .... his old one.
3 Travelling by train is cheaper .... travelling by plane.
4 These sunglasses are .... most popular brand .... all.
5 My daughter is one of .... cleverest students .... her class.
6 This church is .... oldest church .... the city.
7 My sister Sally is .... youngest ....my family.

91

10 Write the comparative and superlative forms of the following adjectives, as in the example.

ADJECTIVE	COMPARATIVE	SUPERLATIVE
sad	........*sadder*........	.....*the saddest*.....
lovely	....	....
much	....	....
bad	....	....
healthy	....	....
amazing	....	....
intelligent	....	....
long	....	....
expensive	....	....
poor	....	....

11 Put the adjectives into the comparative or superlative form, as in the example.

1 It was ...*the deepest*... **(deep)** lake I have ever swum in.
2 Your lecture on Modern Art was .... **(interest)** than mine.
3 *Titanic* was one of .... **(success)** films of the 1990's.
4 Of all the students at my school, Penny is .... **(popular)**.
5 That rock concert was .... **(bad)** I've ever been to.
6 Which is .... **(high)** mountain in the world?
7 My puppy is .... **(young)** than yours.
8 Little Angie is .... **(quiet)** baby I know.

12 Compare and contrast the two hotels using comparative and superlative forms, as in the example.

	The King Hotel	The Rose Hotel
Rooms:	comfortable ***	comfortable **
Maid Service:	good ***	good ***
Room Service:	fast **	fast ***
Prices:	expensive ***	expensive **
Location:	convenient **	convenient ***

*The rooms at the King Hotel are **more comfortable than** the rooms at the Rose Hotel.*
*The rooms at the Rose Hotel are **not as comfortable as** the rooms at the King Hotel.*
*The rooms at the Rose Hotel are **less comfortable than** the rooms at the King Hotel.*

Expressing Preference

13 Put the verbs in brackets into the correct form, as in the example.

1 I'd rather ...*swim*... **(swim)** in the sea than ...*ski*... **(ski)** in the mountains.
2 I prefer .... **(sleep)** in a hotel to .... **(sleep)** in a tent.
3 He would prefer .... **(watch)** TV rather than .... **(go)** to the party.
4 Jeff would rather .... **(go)** out than .... **(stay)** in.
5 They prefer .... **(walk)** to work to .... **(take)** a taxi.
6 Helen would rather .... **(make)** her own clothes than .... **(buy)** them.
7 Frank prefers .... **(play)** chess to .... **(listen)** to music.
8 We would prefer .... **(paint)** the house ourselves rather than .... **(pay)** someone else to do it.

Revision: **Units 1 - 19**

Multiple Choice

14 Choose the correct item.

1 Eating fruit is less fattening .... eating chocolate.
  A of **B** than **C** in

2 How .... bottles of water do we need?
  A some **B** much **C** many

3 He finds cockroaches .... disgusting that he screams whenever he sees one.
  A so **B** such **C** such a

4 You locked the front door, ...?
  A won't you **B** didn't you **C** aren't you

5 I'll never forget .... to Brazil. It was fantastic.
  A go **B** to go **C** going

6 The plants .... watered.
  A is needing **B** need to be **C** need

7 Allan had .... for half an hour when it started to rain.
  A swam **B** been swimming **C** swim

Countable/Uncountable Nouns - Some/Any/No - Much/Many - (A) few/(A) little - Comparative/Superlative Form - Expressing Preference

19

8 Did he .... cry a lot when he was a baby?
   A get used to   **B** use to   **C** used to

9 My village .... a lot since I was a child.
   A has changed   **B** change   **C** is changing

10 He has .... posted the letters.
   A yet   **B** already   **C** since

11 Ed is the man .... wife is a doctor.
   A which   **B** who's   **C** whose

12 *The X-Files* is one of .... most successful programmes on TV.
   A in   **B** the   **C** of

13 My parents .... on a safari last year.
   A had gone   **B** is going   **C** went

14 I will mop the floor .... the children leave for school.
   A until   **B** as soon as   **C** unless

15 A: Would you like some more soup?
   B: Just ...., please.
   A a little   **B** a few   **C** little

Key Word Transformation

15 **Complete each sentence with two to five words, including the word in bold.**

1 She started taking flute lessons ten months ago.
   has   She .... flute lessons for ten months.

2 The Mexican restaurant is more expensive than the Italian one.
   less   The Italian restaurant .... the Mexican one.

3 "Have you eaten snails before?" she asked us.
   if   She asked .... snails before.

4 It was such a funny film that everyone in the cinema laughed.
   so   The film .... in the cinema laughed.

5 People expect she will win the award for best actress.
   expected   She .... the award for best actress.

6 Dad made me mow the lawn this morning.
   was   I .... the lawn this morning.

7 This is an unusual plant. It comes from Africa.
   which   This is an .... from Africa.

8 You shouldn't go out with wet hair.
   were   If I .... go out with wet hair.

9 The cake was so delicious that I asked for the recipe.
   such   It was .... I asked for the recipe.

10 Pam and Debbie are equally imaginative.
   as   Debbie is .... Pam.

11 "I'll meet you outside the bank," Jan said to George.
   told   Jan .... meet him outside the bank.

12 "We've decided to get married," Kate said.
   decided   Kate said .... to get married.

13 Harry isn't small enough to climb through the hole.
   big   Harry .... climb through the hole.

14 It's the first time they have seen snow.
   never   They .... snow before.

15 "Don't open the oven door," Shirley said to Becky.
   to   Shirley ....the oven door.

Error Correction

16 **Cross out the unnecessary word.**

1 He is much more taller than his father.
2 Karen is a dancer who she lives in New York.
3 My parents always go on holiday in the August.
4 I think David is the nicest man I've ever been met.
5 My sister is the taller than me.
6 She won't forgive you unless you will call her and apologise.
7 Becky is as much clever as Stella.
8 This is the most best film I've ever seen.
9 I prefer cooking than to ironing.
10 If you will need me, give me a call.

Tenses of the Infinitive

The infinitive has four tenses in the active and two in the passive.

	Active	Passive
Present	(to) write	(to) be written
Present Cont.	(to) be writing	——
Perfect	(to) have written	(to) have been written
Perfect Cont.	(to) have been writing	

- **present infinitive** — present or future
  *He wants **to have** a party on Saturday.*
- **present continuous infinitive** — an action happening now
  *He is thought **to be living** in France.*
- **perfect infinitive** — refers to the past and shows that the action of the infinitive happened before the action of the verb.
  *They claim **to have met** the President.*
- **perfect continuous infinitive** — refers to the past and emphasises the duration of the action of the infinitive, which happened before the action of the verb.
  *He looks tired. He must **have been working** very hard.*

Note: The perfect infinitive is used with verbs such as **seem, believe, know, appear, claim, expect** and **modal verbs**.

The verb tenses corresponding to the tenses of the infinitive are as follows:

Verb tenses	Infinitive
he gives / will give	➡ (to) give
he is giving / will be giving	➡ (to) be giving
he gave / has given / had given / will have given	➡ (to) have given
he was giving / has been giving / had been giving / will have been giving	➡ (to) have been giving

Making deductions

Must — positive deductions (I'm sure)
- **must + present infinitive** (present/future)
  *They **must be** very happy. They've won first prize.*
- **must + perfect infinitive** (past)
  *He **must have been** on holiday. He's very brown.*

Can't — negative deductions (I'm sure you aren't)
- **can't + present infinitive** (present/future)
  *She **can't be** a nurse. She works for a law firm.*
- **can't + perfect infinitive** (past)
  *She **can't have cooked** the meal. She hates cooking.*

May/Might/Could — possibility (It is possible/perhaps)
- **may/might/could + present infinitive** (present/future)
  *Megan **may bake** a cake on Sunday.*
- **may/might/could + perfect infinitive** (past)
  *Tom **might have forgotten** your phone number.*

Tenses of the Infinitive - Making Deductions

1 Write the corresponding form of the infinitive, as in the example.

1 he wrote .... *(to) have written* ....
2 it is believed ....
3 they are talking ....
4 he will arrive ....
5 she had cleaned ....
6 he was ironing ....
7 they have slept ....
8 it was made ....
9 he had cooked ....
10 it was built ....

2 Fill in *may/might*, *must* or *can't*, as in the example.

1 Kelly's hair looks fantastic. She ...*must*... have dyed it.
2 Dave ...*can't*..... be at home. He's still on holiday.
3 I saw James leave the burning building. He *may* .... be the person who started the fire.
4 Jill ...*can't*........... have invited Fiona to her party. They don't speak to one another.
5 They ...*must*....... have left together as I saw them get into the same car.
6 It ...*might*.... rain this afternoon as it's very cloudy.
7 I went to Sam's house but nobody was there. He ...*must*..... have gone to the office.
8 Look! The door's unlocked. Susan ...*must*.... have forgotten to lock it.

3 Write the appropriate form of the infinitive, as in the example.

1 She can't ...*have taken*... **(take)** an aspirin. She still has a headache.
2 She must .... **(arrive)** at the office by now.
3 They can't .... **(live)** in a flat. They own a house.
4 She must .... **(be)** very successful. She's on the cover of three magazines this month.
5 He looks sad. He must .... **(have)** some bad news.
6 Lilian can't .... **(finish)** her homework. She only started it ten minutes ago.
7 The house could .... **(burn down)** if the fire brigade hadn't arrived on time.
8 He must .... **(hurt)** his leg. He's limping.
9 Lynn can't .... **(be)** at home. She's gone shopping.
10 Julie wasn't at home this morning. She might .... **(go)** to the dentist's.

4 Complete the sentences using *must* or *can't*, as in the examples.

1 John has a good job. (graduate university)
He must have graduated from university.
2 His eyes are red. (go to bed early)
He can't have gone to bed early.
3 Sue is late for work. (oversleep)
....
4 Cathy is wet. (take her umbrella)
....
5 Tina and Bob are relaxed. (have a good holiday)
....
6 Sam is tired. (stay at office late)
....

7 His coat is here. (be upstairs)
....
8 Their dishes are dirty. (eat dinner here)
....
9 Jessica hasn't eaten all day. (be hungry)
....
10 Helen's hair is short. (grow it)
....

5 Complete the following sentences using *must*, *can't*, or *may/might/could*, as in the example.

1 They ....*must*........ be outside.
2 They .... be camping.
3 It .... be very warm.
4 They .... be teenagers.
5 They .... be friends.
6 They .... be enjoying themselves.
7 They .... be on holiday.
8 It .... be summer.

6 Match the questions to the answers and make deductions using *must* or *can't*, as in the example.

1 Has she been working in the garden?
2 Did he graduate from university?
3 Have they been cooking?
4 Are they back from their holiday?
5 Did they have a good time at the party?
6 Did he pay the bill?

a Yes. The kitchen smells wonderful.
b Yes. They stayed until four o'clock in the morning.
c No. No one's at home.
d Yes. Her clothes are dirty.
e No. The telephone has been cut off.
f No. He hasn't got a degree.

(1-d) *She must have been working in the garden because her clothes are dirty.*

7 Look at the pictures and fill in *must*, *can't*, or *may/might/could*. What other deductions can you make for each picture?

1 They ....*must*.... be proud of themselves.

2 She ....*must*.... have lost her way.

3 This place ....*can't*.... be a school.

4 He ....*can't*.... be teaching Maths.

8 Complete each sentence with two to five words, including the word in bold.

1 I'm sure he didn't steal the money.
stolen He ...*can't have stolen*... the money.

2 I'm certain they've arrived by now.
must They ....*must have*.... ....*arrived*.... by now.

3 Perhaps she was having a shower when you rang her.
been She ....*may have been*.... .... a shower when you rang her.

4 I'm sure they are still at home.
be They ....*must be*.... .... at home.

5 It's possible that he forgot to reserve a table.
could He .... a table.

6 I'm sure she didn't know about the surprise party.
have She .... the surprise party.

7 Perhaps he will call you from the airport.
might He ....*might*.... .... the airport.

8 I'm certain she didn't go to work last Saturday.
gone She .... work last Saturday.

Revision: Units 1 - 20

9 Cross out the unnecessary word.

1 The Maths is a very interesting subject.
2 He can't to have seen Stella; she's abroad.
3 She prefers skiing rather to swimming.
4 The Jones are the richer than the Smiths.
5 There is not nobody in the garden.
6 Can I have some of water, please?
7 He's too tired for to go to the party.
8 Jane may have been told him the news.
9 He's going out so to buy some cakes.
10 If I were you, I wouldn't have go to her party.

10 Choose the correct item.

1 A: Can I help you, madam?
   B: Yes, please. I .... for a book on rare birds.
   A looked **B am looking** C look

2 That's the man .... son won a gold medal in the Olympics.
   A which B who's **C whose**

3 I have .... Madrid twice.
   A been to B gone to C go to

4 I will have finished the book .... next week.
   A until **B by** C by the time

5 They .... eat a lot of junk food when they were at university.
   A used to B use to C using to

6 You .... always wear your seat belt when driving a car.
   A mustn't B needn't **C must**

7 Five years .... my father was the mayor of our town.
   A since **B ago** C before

8 Richard .... me that he had a bad cold.
A asked　　　B told　　　C said

9 I .... on the beach at this time tomorrow.
A will be lying　　B will lie　　C am lying

10 I .... a gorgeous silk scarf for my birthday.
A am giving　　B is given　　C was given

11 The windows .... cleaning.
A needs to be　　B need　　C needs

12 Mary was wet because she .... in the rain.
A is walking　　B had been walking　　C walk

13 The new shopping complex .... six months ago.
A is building　　B was built　　C is built

14 Excuse me, could you .... me the way to the station, please?
A say　　B tell　　C ask

15 If I were you, I .... go to bed early.
A would　　B must　　C will

Key Word Transformation

11 **Complete each sentence with two to five words, including the word in bold.**

1 I'm sure they bought a new car last month.
must　　　They .... *must have bell bought* car last month.

2 Mount Everest is higher than Mount Fuji.
as　　　Mount Fuji *isn't as high or* Mount Everest.

3 This watch was less expensive than John's and Jane's watches.
least　　　This watch *was the least expensive* of all.

4 If you don't wear your glasses, your eyes will get tired.
unless　　Your eyes will get tired *unless you wear* glasses.

5 The shoes were so small that they didn't fit me.
too　　　The shoes *were too small for* me to wear.

6 "Don't be late for school," Michelle said to Bruce.
to　　　Michelle told Bruce *not to be late* for school.

7 "When are you leaving for your camping trip?" Ben asked them.
were　　Ben asked *when they were leaving* for their camping trip.

8 It's a year since I last wrote to him.
for　　　I haven't *written to him for* a year.

9 I'm sure they didn't catch the 5am train.
can't　　They *can't have caught* the 5am train.

Word Formation

12 **Fill in the gaps with the correct words derived from the words in bold.**

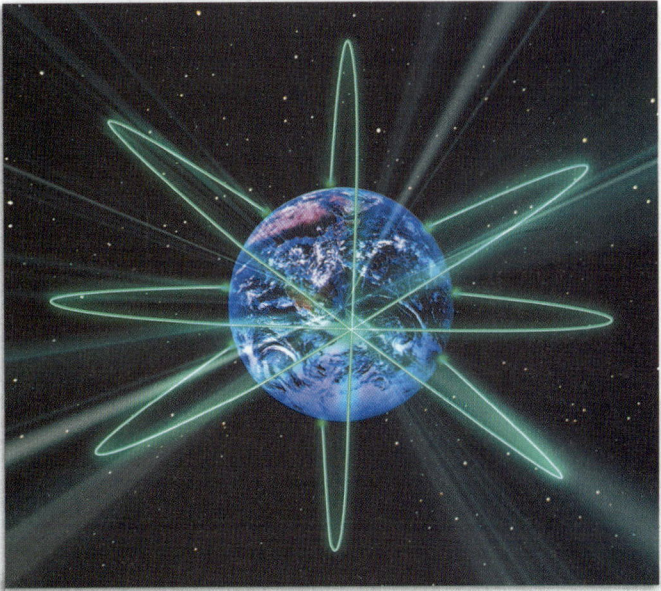

In the future our lives might be very 1) *different* from today. Advances in technology will 2) *probably* make our lives easier and more 3) *interesting*. Computers will be more 4) *useful* than ever and may even replace people in certain jobs. It doesn't take much 5) *imagination* to picture factories without workers and buses without 6) *drivers*. Services will never be 7) *unreliable* again because everything will be done by robots.

Travel, housing and medicine will be much more 8) *advanced* in the future. We may use strange means of transport or live in space-age houses and a cure for every 9) *illness* in the world may have been found by 10) *researching*. Some of these changes are good, but others may prove to be the opposite.

DIFFER
PROBABLE
INTEREST
USE
IMAGINE
DRIVE
RELIABLE
ADVANCE
ILL
RESEARCH

Present and Past Participles

- We use the **present participle (the infinitive of the verb + -ing)** to describe what somebody or something is. It answers the question: "What kind?"
  *She is a very **caring** woman. (What kind of woman? Caring.)*
  *The film was extremely **boring**. (What kind of film? Boring.)*
- We use the **past participle (the infinitive of the verb + ed/d or the irregular past participle form)** to describe how someone feels. It answers the question: "How do you feel?"
  *They were **exhausted** after travelling for ten hours. (How did they feel? Exhausted.)*

Expressing Preference

We use **would/'d rather** (= I'd prefer to) to express preference.

- When the subject of **would rather** is also the subject of the verb that follows, we use:

would/ 'd rather	**present infinitive without to** (present/future reference) ***I'd rather live** in a large city than in a small village.*
	perfect infinitive without to (past reference) ***We'd rather have gone** to France last winter.*

- When the subject of **would rather** is different from the subject of the verb that follows, we use:

would/ 'd rather	**past simple** (present/future reference) ***I'd rather you did** the shopping today.*
	past perfect (past reference) ***I'd rather Kate had called** first.*

We can express preference in other ways:
- **prefer + -ing form/noun + to + -ing form/noun** (general preference)
  *I **prefer walking** to work **to taking** public transport. He **prefers newspapers to magazines**.*
- **prefer + full infinitive + rather than + infinitive without to** (general preference)
  *He **prefers to go** to the cinema rather than **go** to the theatre.*
- **would prefer + full infinitive + rather than + (infinitive without to)** (specific preference)
  *She **would prefer to eat** at a restaurant today **rather than (eat)** at home.*
- **would rather + infinitive without to + than + (infinitive without to)**
  *I **would rather drive** a car **than (drive)** a lorry.*

Expressing Positive or Negative Agreement

- We use **so** to agree with a positive statement.
  so + auxiliary verb + subject
  A: I love watching comedies.
  *B: **So do I.***
  A: I had a wonderful day today.
  *B: **So did I.***
- We use **neither/nor** to agree with a negative statement.
  neither/nor + auxiliary verb + subject
  A: I don't like Brussels sprouts.
  *B: **Neither do I.***
  A: I won't go on the picnic because I'm ill.
  *B: **Nor will I.***

Present and Past Participles

1 Underline the correct word, as in the example.

1 A: Did Bill like his birthday present?
   B: Oh, yes. He was **thrilling/thrilled** with it.
2 A: How's your new job?
   B: It's great but it's a bit **tired/tiring**.
3 A: Did you enjoy the film?
   B: No, not at all. I found it very **confusing/confused**.
4 A: How do you feel after being away from work for a month?
   B: Wonderful! I feel really **relaxed/relaxing**.
5 A: Was Peter late for dinner again?
   B: Yes, and I was very **annoying/annoyed** because he didn't call to tell me.
6 A: Did you have a good swim?
   B: I had a marvellous swim. It was very **refreshed/refreshing**.
7 A: Did you meet Mr Grant?
   B: Yes. What an **interesting/interested** person he is!
8 A: Have you heard the news? Ken crashed his car.
   B: Yes, I heard. I'm **amazing/amazed** that he wasn't hurt.
9 A: Did you read the book I lent you?
   B: Yes, I found the main character very **charming/charmed**.
10 A: How are the twins?
   B: They're very **exciting/excited** about opening their gifts tomorrow morning.

2 Fill in the correct form of the word in bold, as in the example.

1 Your trip to Los Angeles sounds *...fascinating....* . **(fascinate)**
2 I didn't like the film because it was ....boring.......... . **(bore)**
3 Everyone thinks Emily is an ....amusing............ person. **(amuse)**
4 They were ....thrilled...... to hear that their daughter was getting married. **(thrill)**

5 I was ....shocked....... to find out that Thomas had left his job. **(shock)**
6 What's the most ....embarrassing....... thing you've ever done? **(embarrass)**
7 The children were so ....frightened........ by the story that they couldn't sleep. **(frighten)**
8 I have had such an ....exhausting......... day that all I want to do is to go to bed. **(exhaust)**

Expressing Preference

3 Fill in the correct form of the verbs in brackets, as in the example.

1 I prefer ....meeting........ **(meet)** my friends rather than ......playing...... **(play)** video games.
2 Debbie would rather ....stay........ **(stay)** at home than ......go......... **(go)** to the cinema.
3 I would prefer ....to read....... **(read)** the book rather than ......see...... **(see)** the film.
4 Bill would rather ....read....... **(read)** a book than ....write......... **(write)** a letter.
5 We'd rather ....see....... **(see)** the football match live than ......watch...... **(watch)** it on TV.
6 They prefer ....baking....... **(bake)** their own bread to ......buying...... **(buy)** it from the shop.
7 I'd rather Becky ......travelled...... **(travel)** by train than by plane.
8 I'd rather Sue and Frank .... **(clean)** the garage yesterday.
9 Arnold prefers ....working....... **(work)** on his computer to ......talking...... **(talk)** on the phone.
10 I prefer ....exercising....... **(exercise)** at the gym rather than ......jogging...... **(jog)** in the park.
11 They'd rather ....buy....... **(buy)** a second-hand camera than a brand new one.
12 I'd rather you ....go...... **(go)** to bed right away.
13 We'd rather ....live....... **(live)** on the sixth floor than on the ground floor.
14 I'd rather Tom .... **(visit)** his grandmother last night.

4 In pairs, use the the prompts below to ask and answer questions, as in the examples.

1 rather spend the day at the beach or at the park?
A: ...*Would you rather spend the day at the beach or at the park?*...
B: ...*I'd rather spend the day at the beach.*...

2 prefer eat ice cream or chocolate cake for dessert?
A: ...*Would you prefer to eat ice cream or chocolate cake for dessert?*...
B: ...*I would prefer to eat chocolate cake rather than ice cream for dessert.*...

3 rather go to the cinema or the theatre?
A: .... ?
B: ....

4 prefer cook dinner or order a takeaway?
A: .... ?
B: ....

5 prefer have boiled potatoes or chips with your meal?
A: ....?
B: ....

6 rather wash the dishes or dry them?
A: ....?
B: ....

7 rather take a computer course or a Spanish course?
A: ....?
B: ....

8 prefer do the shopping or the ironing?
A: ....?
B: ....

5 Fill in the gaps with *prefer, would prefer* or *would rather*, as in the example.

1 I ...*prefer*... painting to drawing.
2 He .... drink milk than drink orange juice.
3 We .... going camping to staying in the city.
4 We .... go by car than take the bus.
5 I .... antique furniture to modern furniture.
6 .... you .... to eat at home or go to a restaurant tonight?
7 She .... study Art History than Economics.
8 .... they .... to stay in a hotel or in a guest house?
9 He .... fix his motorcycle than take it to the mechanic.
10 I .... reading books to reading newspapers.

6 Complete each sentence with two to five words, including the word in bold.

1 I like playing chess but I love playing backgammon.
to I .... chess.
2 I would rather have my own business than work for someone else.
prefer I would .... business rather than work for someone else.
3 They'd rather go camping than skiing.
rather They prefer .... go skiing.
4 I like listening to classical music more than rock music.
to I .... rock music.
5 I would rather own a house than rent one.
prefer I would .... rather than rent one.
6 We like going to the opera more than the theatre.
to We .... the theatre.

Expressing Positive or Negative Agreement

7 Respond to the statements, as in the example.

1 A: I haven't been to the funfair.
B: ...*Neither/Nor have I.*...
2 A: I love watching music videos.
B: ....
3 A: I didn't know it was Bob's birthday.
B: ....
4 A: I went to the annual picnic yesterday.
B: ....
5 A: I really liked the latest *Star Wars* film.
B: ....

6 A: I don't like soap operas.
B: ....

7 A: I didn't go to Jane's party on Friday night.
B: ....

8 A: I really want to go to the Spice Girls concert.
B: ....

9 A: I love horses.
B: ....

10 A: I was late for school this morning.
B: ....

Revision: Units 1 - 14

Multiple Choice

8 **Choose the correct item.**

1 I'd rather eat fresh vegetables .... eat meat.
A prefer   **B** to   **C** than

2 Fred must .... now.
A be sleeping   **B** have slept   **C** sleep

3 Catherine is one .... the most beautiful women I know.
A of   **B** in   **C** than

4 There aren't .... eggs left.
A no   **B** any   **C** some

5 I'll take my scarf so that I .... get cold.
A can   **B** wouldn't   **C** won't

6 .... elephants and bears are mammals.
A Both   **B** None   **C** Neither

7 I forgot .... my alarm clock last night so I woke up late.
A to set   **B** setting   **C** set

8 *Dracula* was .... by Bram Stoker.
A write   **B** written   **C** wrote

9 Janet .... finished all her homework by six o'clock.
A will have   **B** will   **C** has

10 If I were you, I .... go to the dentist.
A will   **B** would have   **C** would

Error Correction

9 **Cross out the unnecessary word.**

1 He stopped to smoking two years ago.

2 I have always wanted to study the medicine.

3 I'm be going to the art exhibition on Sunday.

4 You mustn't to run in the corridors.

5 I've been taking aerobics classes for since eight months.

6 This is the man who I bought the computer from him.

Key Word Transformation

10 **Complete each sentence with two to five words, including the word in bold.**

1 1998 was the year I got my degree.
which   1998 .... I got my degree.

2 It's ages since I went dancing.
haven't   I .... ages.

3 The story was so sad that I couldn't stop crying.
such   It was .... I couldn't stop crying.

4 Monica hasn't eaten pizza for three months.
ate   The last time .... three months ago.

5 I don't spend as much money on clothes as Stacey does.
than   Stacey spends .... I do.

6 You can't leave the table if you don't eat all your vegetables.
unless   You can't leave the table .... vegetables.

7 "You took my credit card," she said to Keith.
accused   She .... her credit card.

8 I would rather drink tea than drink coffee.
prefer   I would .... than drink coffee.

Word Formation

11 **Fill in the gaps with the correct words derived from the words in bold.**

Are you an **1)** .... person? **ADVENTURE**
Would you like to go on an **2)** .... **USUAL** holiday this summer? If the answers to these questions are yes, then you should book a safari holiday with WILDTIMES.
We offer you the opportunity to see animals in their **3)** .... **NATURE** habitat in the heart of Africa. You can spend an **4)** .... month **EXCITE** travelling around the country where you will see both **5)** .... **AMAZE** animals and **6)** .... views. **IMPRESS**
Our **7)** .... tour guides will **EXPERIENCE** provide you with **8)** .... facts **INTEREST** about the African wildlife. The hotels we use have very **9)** .... rooms, **COMFORT** and are not very **10)** .... **EXPENSE**
A safari holiday will be one of the most **11)** .... experiences of your **ENJOY** life. For more **12)** ...., **INFORM** please call 0800 662823.

Causative Form

- We use **have + object + past participle** to say that we arranged for someone to do something for us.
Sue hired a painter to paint the house → **Sue had the house painted.** (She didn't paint it herself—the painter did it.)
- The order of words (i.e. **have + object + past participle**) must not be changed because if it is, the meaning of the sentence will be changed.
He had the tyres changed. = *He employed someone to change the tyres.* **But:** *He had changed the tyres.* = *He (himself) changed the tyres.*
- Questions and negations are formed with **do/does** in the present simple and **did** in the past simple.
Do you **have your hair cut** *every six months? I* **didn't have the fence painted** *last week.*

Study the following:

Present Simple	She **makes** her clothes.	She **has her clothes made**.
Present Continuous	She **is making** her clothes.	She **is having her clothes made**.
Past Simple	She **made** her clothes.	She **had her clothes made**.
Past Continuous	She **was making** her clothes.	She **was having her clothes made**.
Future Simple	She **will make** her clothes.	She **will have her clothes made**.
Present Perfect	She **has made** her clothes.	She **has had her clothes made**.
Infinitive	She **must make** her clothes.	She **must have her clothes made**.

- We can also use **causative form** to express that something unpleasant happened to someone.
Tom **had his house burgled** *last month. (= Tom's house was burgled. This unpleasant incident happened to him.)*

Causative Form

1 **Complete the sentences by putting the verb *have* into the correct form, as in the example.**

1 Emily ...*has*... her newspaper delivered every morning by her neighbour's son.
2 The Campbells ...are having... their kitchen painted at the moment.
3 I ...had... my hair cut short last week because I needed a change.
4 He ...has... his car serviced by the mechanic next Tuesday.
5 She ...had... her carpets fitted yesterday when I called.
6 I ...have... just ...had... my picture taken by a professional photographer.
7 Mark ...will have... some apple trees planted in a week's time.
8 Steve ...had... his wallet stolen while he was doing the shopping.
9 I ...am having... my jeans shortened tomorrow.
10 I always ...have... my rubbish collected on Fridays.

2 **Each of the following people had something unpleasant happen to them last week. Make sentences using *the causative form,* as in the example.**

1 Meg (her flat/break into) by burglars.
   ...*Meg had her flat broken into by burglars.*...

2 Gary (his motorcycle/steal) from outside the disco.
....

3 The MacDoyles (basement/flood) by heavy rain.
....

4 Robin (her favourite dress/tear) by her friend.
....

5 Thomas (his CD player/break) by his little brother.
....

6 Neil (house/strike) by lightning.
....

7 Mary (window/smash) by a ball.
....

8 Charles (car/damage) by a falling tree.
....

3 **Rewrite the following sentences in the causative form, as in the example.**

1 Holly is going to ask the seamstress to sew her dress.
   ...*She is going to have her dress sewn (by the seamstress).*...

2 Someone has tidied the garden for Mark.
....
....

3 When will they fix his telephone?
....
....

4 Pat pays someone to clean the windows every week.
....
....

5 Can you tell someone to move those boxes?
....
....

6 When will they deliver Dan's sofa?
....
....

7 Sally is going to ask the travel agent to book the tickets.
....
....

8 Howard should ask someone to deliver the package.
....
....

9 When will you service the car?
....
....

10 Pay someone to make the curtains for you.
....
....

11 Someone has shortened Alison's skirt.
....
....

12 Doug is going to ask the bank to pay some bills for him.
....
....

4 **Jennifer Baker is a successful businesswoman who has many things done for her. Look at the notes below and make sentences, as in the example.**

1 hair/cut (by her personal hairdresser)
   ...*She has her hair cut by her personal hairdresser.*...

2 nails/paint (by a manicurist)
....

3 shopping/do (by her housekeeper)
....

4 telephone/answer (by her secretary)
....

5 letters/type (by her secretary)
....

6 appointments/make (by her secretary)
....

7 fresh flowers/deliver to her office every morning (by the florist)
....

8 house/clean (by a cleaner)
....

5 Tommy Davis is a local singer. Freddy Marble is a famous rock star. Tommy does everything himself while Freddy arranges for other people to do things for him. Write sentences about Freddy, as in the example.

Tommy Davis

1 I write the words for my songs.
2 I answer my own letters.
3 I prepare my meals every day.
4 I arrange my own shows.
5 I book my hotel rooms.
6 I carry my equipment myself.

Freddy Marble

1 *...I have the words for my songs written....*
2 *I have my letters answered*
3 *I have my meals prepared*
4 *I have my shows arranged*
5 *I have my hotel rooms booked*
6 *I have my equipment carried*

6 Becky is a chef at a popular restaurant. Look at the list below and say whether she does the following things or she has somebody else do them for her.

1 clean the kitchen (staff)
   ...She has the kitchen cleaned by her staff....
2 organise the menu (Becky)
   She has the menu organised by
3 order the supplies (Becky)
   She has the supplies ordered by Becky
4 wash the vegetables (staff)
   She has the vegetables washed by her
5 prepare the meals (Becky)
   She has the meals prepared by Becky

6 taste the food (Becky)
   She has the food tasted by Becky
7 do the dishes (staff)
   She has the dishes done by her
8 take out the rubbish (staff)
   She has the rubbish taken out by her staff

7 Study the situations, then write the answers using the causative form, as in the example.

1 Jane is going to the hairdresser's tomorrow. What's she going to do?
   ...She's going to have her hair cut....
2 Rob's suit is dirty. What should he do?
   ....
3 Mandy's wedding dress was made especially for her. What did she have done?
   ....
4 Chris has paid the mechanic for repairing his motorcycle. What has he done?
   ....
5 Tim's bedroom walls are dirty. Painting them would help. What should he do?
   ....
6 The tap in their bathroom is leaking. What should they do?
   ....

Revision: Units 1 - 22

Error Correction

8 **Cross out the unnecessary word.**

1 You'll get wet unless you not take an umbrella.
2 I spent all weekend at the home.
3 If they will call, I'll invite them to dinner.
4 This novel was being written by Charles Dickens.
5 Your hair is much more longer than mine.
6 Who did won the competition?
7 My mother made me to clean my room.
8 The children love to going to the circus.
9 The girl who she is my best friend is called Mary.
10 You'd better to see a doctor.
11 They don't mind going to bed late, do they not?
12 He prefers playing squash rather than to playing tennis.
13 She told to me she would be late.

Multiple Choice

9 Choose the correct item.

1 Fred .... the house two hours ago.
   A is leaving   **B** left   **C** has left

2 If you .... any assistance, I'll be happy to help you.
   A need   **B** will need   **C** needed

3 My brother has never .... to Argentina.
   A gone   **B** go   **C** been

4 Maria isn't here. She's .... to the post office.
   A gone   **B** been   **C** going

5 I haven't seen Andy .... the last day of school.
   A yet   **B** for   **C** since

6 I .... up the stairs when the accident happened.
   A went   **B** have gone   **C** was going

7 He has .... fixed the computer.
   A already   **B** yet   **C** since

8 I'm very thirsty. I think I .... a glass of water.
   A 'm having   **B** 'm going to have   **C** 'll have

9 She asked us who .... broken the vase.
   A have   **B** had   **C** is having

10 I'd rather .... a book than play golf.
   A read   **B** to read   **C** reading

11 A: I don't want to watch TV.
    B: .... do I.
   A Not   **B** So   **C** Neither

12 "You are coming to the party, ...?"
   A aren't you   **B** will you   **C** won't you

13 Janet will have finished cooking .... seven o'clock.
   A since   **B** until   **C** by

14 I don't mind .... to work.
   A walk   **B** walking   **C** to walk

15 That's the woman .... photograph was in the newspaper.
   A whose   **B** who's   **C** which

16 Oh no! I .... my wallet.
   A have lost   **B** had lost   **C** am losing

17 When .... you start learning Italian?
   A have   **B** did   **C** had

Key Word Transformation

10 Complete each sentence with two to five words, including the word in bold.

1 We last went to the cinema two months ago.
   for   We haven't ..... *been to the cin* .... *for* ..... two months.

2 I'm sure he has finished typing the letters.
   must   He ..... *must be finis* .... *typing* ..... the letters.

3 They'd rather go on a package holiday than arrange their own holiday.
   rather   They'd prefer to go on a ..... *packen* ..... *holiday than arrange* .... *than* ..... their own holiday.

4 Perhaps she is at home now.
   may   She ..... *may be at hmo* .... now.

5 Fiona is kinder than Karen.
   as   Karen ..... *isn't kinder as* ..... Fiona.

6 I should hire a photographer. I want someone to take my picture.
   to   I should hire ....
   ..... picture.

7 She is too young to be out so late at night.
   not   She ..... *is so old may to* ..... be out so late at night.

8 I regret not calling you.
   wish   I ..... *wish I haven call* ..... you.

Word Formation

11 Fill in the gaps with the correct words derived from the words in bold.

Dear Steve,

How are you? I'm writing to tell you some **1)** ..... *amazing* ..... news. **AMAZE**
You know how much I've always wanted to be an **2)** ..... *actor* ..... . Well, my dream **ACT**
has **3)** ..... *finally* ..... come true. Last **FINAL**
week, I was chosen to play the lead role in the **4)** ..... *famou* ..... play by Shakespeare, **FAME**
King Lear, at Chatsworth Theatre. I'm extremely **5)** ..... *nervous* ..... about the **NERVE**
whole thing but **6)** ..... *lucky* ..... **LUCK**
I've got a great drama teacher. Anyway, the performance is on Saturday, 5th November. I hope you can be there.

Yours,
Sam

look after:	to take care of sb/sth
look for:	to try to find, to search for sb/sth
look forward to:	to expect sth with pleasure
look up:	to try to find a word, name, number, etc. in a reference book

1 Fill in the correct particle(s).

1 If you're not sure how to spell a word, **look** it .... in the dictionary.
2 Who's going to **look** ...*after*.... the dog while you're on holiday?
3 I can't wait for the camping trip, I'm really **looking** ...*forward to*.... it.
4 Tracy has lost her keys. She's been **looking** ...*for*.... them all morning.
5 When we were young, my grandmother used to **look** ...*after*.... us at the weekends.
6 "Excuse me. I'm **looking** ...*for*.... Mount Street. Could you tell me where it is?"
7 A: How can we find Liz's address?
   B: Let's **look** it ...*up*.... in the phone book.
8 A: Don't you have a dentist's appointment on Monday?
   B: Yes, and I'm not **looking** ...*forward to*.... it at all!

run into sb:	to meet sb by chance
run out of:	to finish; to have no more of sth
run after:	to chase
run over:	to hit sb/sth with a vehicle

2 Fill in the correct particle(s).

1 A: What do you need from the shop?
   B: Well, we've **run** ...*out*.... eggs, so get a dozen.
2 A: What happened to Sam's bicycle? It's in pieces!
   B: It was **run** ...*over*.... by a bus yesterday.
3 Mike threw the football and the dog **ran** ...*after*.... it.
4 A: Have you heard the news? Billy's in town.
   B: Yes, I know. I **ran** ...*into*.... him this morning.
5 The car turned the corner, lost control and **ran** ...*over*.... a dog.
6 I can't do any more sit-ups. I've **run** ...*out*.... energy.
7 The policeman **ran** ...*after*.... the burglar for five minutes before he finally caught him.
8 I **ran** ...*into*.... an old school friend who I hadn't seen for ten years.

break down:	to stop working (cars, engines, etc.)
break into:	to enter a place by force
break out:	to begin suddenly (wars, fires, fights, etc.)
break up:	to stop for holidays (schools, etc.)

3 Fill in the correct particle(s).

1 The fire **broke** .... early this morning and destroyed many buildings in the city centre.
2 School **breaks** ...*up*.... for the summer on June 18.
3 The truck **broke** .... on the motorway and caused a major traffic jam.
4 The jewellery shop on Lewis Street has been **broken** ...*into*.... three times this year.
5 The washing machine is leaking. I hope it doesn't **break** ...*down*....
6 A fight **broke** ...*out*.... after the football match yesterday.
7 When school **broke** ...*up*.... for the Christmas holiday last year, Tom went to Spain.
8 Two men wearing masks **broke** ...*into*.... Boyd's Bank and stole £100,000.

come across:	to find sth by chance
come back:	to return
come round:	to visit
come into:	to inherit sth

4 Fill in the correct particle(s).

1 As I was cleaning my attic I **came** ...*across*.... an old photograph of my grandmother.
2 Bill **came** ...*into*.... a huge amount of money when his cousin died.
3 We are having such a wonderful time here in Barbados, that we'd like to **come** ...*over*.... next summer.
4 Why don't you **come** ...*out*.... for a cup of coffee after work?
5 When Mrs Winston died, her butler **came** ...*into*.... a small fortune.
6 Pete **came** ...*across*.... an antique table in a second-hand shop.
7 My sister **came** ...*round*.... last night and we played cards.
8 When Mr Jenkins **comes** ...*back*.... from lunch, please tell him to call me.

put out:	to stop a fire burning
put sb up:	to provide sb with a place to stay
put on:	to place clothes on one's body, to wear
put off:	to postpone, to arrange for sth to happen at a later time, date, etc.

5 Fill in the correct particle(s).

1 There were no casualties as firefighters managed to **put** ......out.... the fire quickly.
2 She didn't **put** ......on........ her jacket as it wasn't cold outside.
3 My brother came to visit me and I **put** him ......up........ for the night.
4 Due to the storm, I **put** ......off........ my doctor's appointment until the following week.
5 It's past your bedtime! **Put** ......on........ your pyjamas and go to bed!
6 Jenny was too scared to stay home alone while her sister was away, so her friend **put** her ......up........ for the week.
7 Don't forget to **put** ......out........ the fire before you go to bed.
8 Our monthly meeting has been **put** ......off........ until next Wednesday.

turn into:	to change into, to become sb/sth else
turn down:	to refuse an offer, etc.
turn on:	to switch on
turn up:	to arrive

6 Fill in the correct particle(s).

1 I had to **turn** ......down........ Fred's invitation to his party as I'll be out of town that evening.
2 In the famous comic strip, Clark Kent **turns** ......into........ Superman in a phone booth.
3 You'll never guess who **turned** ......up........ at Chris' barbecue yesterday!
4 Could you **turn** ......on........ the air conditioning, please? It's very hot in here.
5 When the princess kissed the ugly frog, he **turned** ......into........ a handsome prince.
6 Vanessa **turned** ......on........ the answering machine before she left the house.
7 James was offered the job, but he **turned** it ......down........ because the salary wasn't very high.
8 Unfortunately, we **turned** ......up........ at the restaurant just as it was closing.

take over:	to take control of sth
take after:	to look like, to behave like
take up:	to begin sth new (a hobby, sport, etc.)
take off:	(of aeroplanes) to leave the ground, to depart

7 Fill in the correct particle(s).

1 My doctor advised me to **take** .... a sport to help me lose weight.
2 Michael is very tidy. In that way, he **takes** .... his father.
3 You should check in two hours before your flight is scheduled to **take** ......off........ .
4 Unfortunately, many small firms are **taken** ......over........ by larger ones.
5 My husband has beautiful blue eyes. I hope our children will **take** ......up........ him.
6 Little Tammy loves dancing and wants to **take** ......up........ ballet.
7 Despite the bad weather, our flight to Chicago still **took** ......off........ on time.
8 While we were sailing my father let me **take** ......over........ the wheel so he could rest.

Revision: Phrasal Verbs

Multiple Choice

8 Choose the correct item.

1 Harry said he wasn't coming to the picnic but he turned .... at the last minute.
A on   B into   **C** up

2 A: Why are you going to the post office?
   B: Because I've run .... of stamps.
   A into   **B** out   C over

3 Our flight was delayed, so the airline company put us .... in a hotel for the night.
   A out   **B** up   C off

4 A fight broke .... just as we were leaving the match.
   A out   B down   C into

5 My father's greengrocer's shop was taken .... by a large supermarket.
   A off   B after   **C** over

107

6 As Michelle was surfing the net, she came .... an interesting website on prehistoric animals.
A into   **B** across   **C** round

7 I am looking .... to hearing from you soon.
A after   **B** up   **C** forward

8 Passengers are not allowed to use their mobile phones while the plane is taking ....
A off   **B** after   **C** over

9 Steve ran .... my skateboard with his motorcycle.
A after   **B** out of   **C** over

10 We put .... our camping trip because Joyce wasn't feeling well.
A off   **B** out   **C** on

9 **Fill in the gaps with the particles in the list below.**

round, after, up, into, on, down, back

1 I have arranged for a babysitter to look after the children on Friday night so we can go out.

2 You'll never guess who's coming up tonight!

3 Mr Stevens was turned down for the position because he didn't have any computer skills.

4 Mrs Stanley will call you when she comes back from Seattle.

5 Randy, who loves extreme sports, has taken up skydiving.

6 A: Do you know when the telescope was invented?
B: No, but we can always look it up in the encyclopaedia.

7 I can't make a copy of this document because the photocopier has broken down.

8 Why don't you turn on the kettle and I'll prepare the sandwiches.

9 We had to break into our house because we had lost our keys.

10 The magician clapped his hand and immediately the flowers turned into a rabbit.

Key Word Transformation

10 **Complete each sentence with two to five words, including the word in bold.**

1 With her gorgeous blue eyes, she really looks like her mother.
takes With her gorgeous blue eyes, she really takes after her mother.

2 Joe met his ex-boss at the conference today.
into Joe came into at the conference today.

3 The puppy was digging holes in the garden, trying to find the bone he had buried.
looking The puppy was digging holes in the garden looking for the bone he had buried.

4 When you go camping, always remember to stop the camp fire from burning before you go to sleep.
out When you go camping, always remember to .... before you go to sleep.

5 "Why didn't the security guard chase the thief?"
run "Why didn't the security guard run after the thief?"

6 Samantha inherited an enormous amount of money when her aunt died last year.
came Samantha came into of money when her aunt died last year.

7 It was such a cold day that I wore my woollen hat and gloves.
on It was such a cold day that I .... and gloves.

8 Do you know when school stops for Easter?
up Do you know when .... up Easter?

9 Cathy's application wasn't accepted because she had very little experience.
turned Cathy's application turned down had very little experience.

11 Underline the correct word.

1 A: Who's going to **look after/run after** Scruffy
when you're away?
B: My Mum is.

2 A fire **put out/broke out** in the west wing of the
library late last night.

3 Kate decided to **take up/look up** Italian lessons
because she wants to live in Venice one day.

4 Caterpillars **come into/turn into** butterflies in the
summer.

5 A: How is your cousin's bookshop doing?
B: Badly, I'm afraid. It was **taken over/run over**
by a bigger company.

6 "**Turn on/Put on** your sun hat if you're going to
the beach," Mum said to me.

7 We've **put off/taken off** our dinner party until
we've finished redecorating the house.

8 The train **turned down/broke down** in the middle
of the mountains.

9 It was so kind of your parents to **break up/put up**
my brother for the weekend.

10 "Did you hear what happened to Mr Wilson? His
house was **run into/broken into** yesterday."

**12 Use the phrasal verbs below in the correct tense
to fill in the blanks.**

*come round, not run out of, come across,
look forward to, look for, come back, take after*

Dear Cindy,

Sorry I haven't written to you for so long but I had
lost your new address. In fact, I **1)** ....
it for more than a month before I finally **2)** ....
.... it.
I hope everything's OK and you **3)** ....
.... energy with all those trips you
have been going on. Things are a bit crazy here as
we're trying to finish redecorating the house because
Susie **4)** .... from hospital with
her new baby, Nicholas, on Tuesday.
Everybody thinks he **5)** ....
his mother because he's got dark eyes and a very
pale complexion. Well, you'll tell us what you think
when you **6)** .... to see him.
As you can imagine, little Nicholas is all we talk
about these days. Anyway, write back soon. I **7)** .....
.... hearing from you.

Love,
Anne

13 Match Column A to Column B.

A		**B**
1 What time does		**A** look it up in the encyclopaedia.
2 They bought a lovely house		**B** if a fire breaks out.
3 If you need more information on Napoleon		**C** because the weather was bad.
4 You are very lucky that you weren't		**D** the plane to Hong Kong take off?
5 All students should know what to do		**E** when they ran into their grandfather.
6 We had to put off the tennis tournament		**F** she never turned up for their meeting.
7 The children were on their way to school		**G** with the money they came into last year.
8 He waited and waited but		**H** run over by the lorry!

**14 Fill in the blanks with the correct verb to
complete the sentences.**

1 I'll make a chocolate cake if you ....
on the oven.

2 John's coming home next week as his school is
.... up for the holidays.

3 "Did you hear that Allen ....
down Emily's invitation to her Christmas party?"

4 The Carltons' dog has run away. They've been
.... for him all night.

5 When I was on holiday in Mexico, I ....
.... into my old school teacher.

6 A: Does this dishwasher have a guarantee?
B: Of course. If it .... down
within the next twelve months, we'll repair it
free of charge.

7 A: Mum, what do firefighters do?
B: Well, they do many things. They ....
.... out fires, rescue people and
save animals.

8 I .... across a gorgeous
antique lamp at the local bazaar.

9 A: Let's have a barbecue tonight.
B: Good idea! But we'll have to go to the shop
because we've .... out of charcoal.

10 A: Now that it's the summer holidays, what are
you going to do with your free time?
B: Well, I've decided to ....
up cycling.

11 A: You don't need to stay in a hotel. We'll ....
.... you up for the night.
B: Thanks very much. I really appreciate it.

109

Place

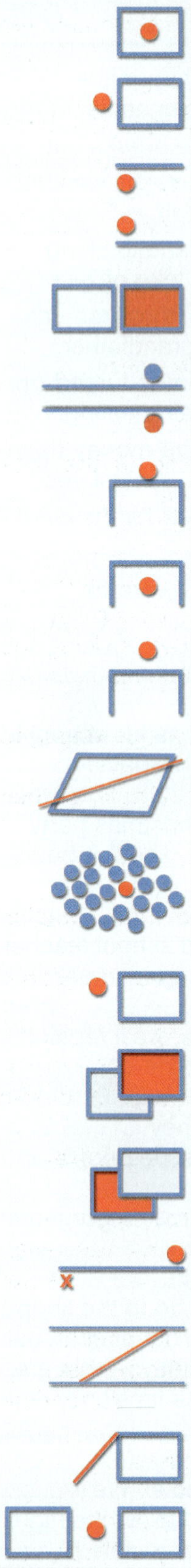

	in/inside
	outside
	below
	above
	next to/by/beside
	opposite
	on
	under
	over
	through
	among
	near
	in front of
	behind
	along
	across
	against
	between

Movement

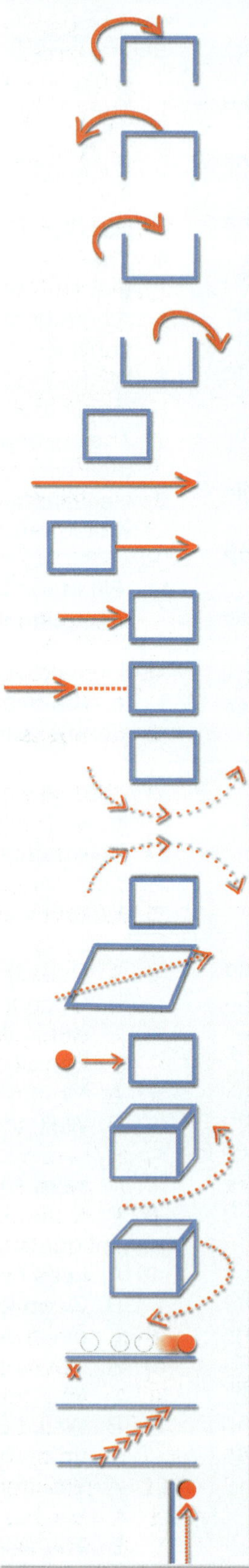

	on/onto
	off
	into
	out of
	past
	from
	to
	towards
	under
	over
	through
	near
	behind
	in front of
	along
	across
	up

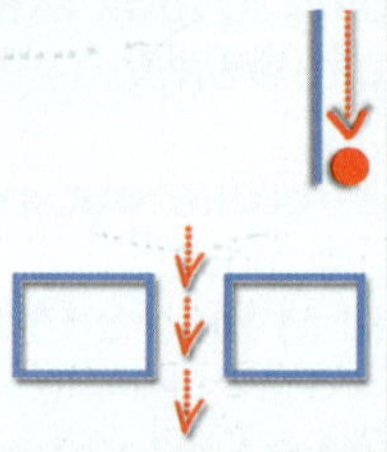

	down
	between

Time

AT

at 2.30, 5.15, etc.
at Christmas/Easter
at noon/night/midnight
at breakfast/lunch/
dinner time, etc.
at that time
at the moment/weekend, etc.

IN

in the morning/afternoon/evening
in the Christmas holiday(s), etc.
in May/September, etc.
in (the) winter/spring, etc.
in 1989/1995, etc.
in the 18th/20th century, etc.
in two/four, etc. hours

ON

on Tuesday/Friday, etc.
on Easter Sunday, Christmas
Day, etc.
on Saturday/Monday, etc. night
on July 15th/May 28th, etc.
on a summer's/winter's day
on that day

Note:
We never use **at, in** or **on**
before **yesterday, next, this,
tomorrow, last, every**.
*She's visiting her mother **this**
Friday.*

1 Underline the correct preposition.

1 Dave's bike is leaning **onto/against** the garage wall.
2 A: Where's Mum?
   B: She's **in/on** the kitchen making an apple pie.
3 The new hotel is **opposite/along** Stanley Park.
4 Julie didn't recognise me. In fact, she walked straight **towards/past** me.
5 A: Do you know where Claire lives?
   B: Yes. Doesn't she live **near/along** the flower shop?
6 I hung the painting **over/up** our bed.
7 Harold sat **outside/next to** Mrs Medley at the dinner party.
8 The cat fell asleep **among/under** the dining room table.
9 The little boy hid **from/behind** a tree and waited for his friend to find him.
10 I'll meet you **towards/outside** the museum at eight o'clock.
11 We walked **between/along** the deserted, sandy beach.
12 A: Why are you so tired?
   B: Because I walked all the way **from/inside** the city centre.

2 Choose the correct item.

1 I parked the car .... the hospital and went inside.
   A under   **B** in front of   **C** towards
2 There was a fallen tree .... the road.
   A outside   **B** against   **C** across
3 There's a river that runs .... my village.
   A across   **B** over   **C** through
4 .... the trees was a charming, little cottage.
   A In   **B** Along   **C** Among
5 My house is .... the bicycle shop and the post office.
   A between   **B** from   **C** among
6 A: What's .... the box?
   B: A diamond necklace.
   A on to   **B** opposite   **C** inside
7 We live on the second floor, ... the newsagent's.
   A above   **B** on   **C** in
8 I walked all the way .... the city centre to the harbour yesterday.
   A above   **B** from   **C** near

9 We got .... the train at Ellington Station.
   A above   **B** off   **C** down
10 On our way .... Joanne's house, we stopped and bought some flowers.
   A to   **B** up   **C** off
11 The mother held out her hands and the baby walked .... her.
   A below   **B** towards   **C** by
12 At night, I always keep a glass of water .... me on my bedside table.
   A beside   **B** under   **C** across

3 Fill in the gaps with _at, in,_ and _on_ where necessary.

1 A: Don't forget that we are going to the rock festival .... Thursday night.
   B: I would never forget the festival!
2 A: What time is the meeting?
   B: It's .... 2.00 .... the afternoon.
3 A: Let's go away .... December.
   B: Good idea! Why don't we go on a skiing trip .... the Christmas holidays.
   A: That's a terrific idea!
4 A: Guess what! Tom and Mary got engaged .... last night.
   B: How wonderful! Have they set a date for their wedding?
   A: Yes, they are getting married .... October.
5 A: When do the children have their Spanish lesson .... this week?
   B: I have arranged for their tutor to come .... Wednesday.
6 A: Mum, when was Grandpa born?
   B: He was born .... May 25th, 1927.
7 A: Are the Smiths going to come over for dinner .... New Year's Eve?
   B: Yes, we are expecting them .... the evening.
8 A: When did you learn to ride a bicycle?
   B: I think it was .... 1990 when I was seven years old. I remember it was .... a hot summer's day.
9 A: When was the first automobile invented?
   B: It was invented .... the 19th century.
10 A: Why don't we meet .... lunchtime .... next Friday.
   B: I'm sorry, I can't. I have a dentist's appointment .... that day.
11 A: Are you going away .... August?
   B: Yes, we go away .... every August.

A

absent from (adj)
according to (prep)
accuse sb of (v)
accustomed to (adj)
advantage of (n)
(but: **there's an advantage in**)
advice on (n)
afraid of (adj)
agree to/on sth (v)

agree with sb (v)
aim at (v)
amazed at/by (adj)
angry about sth (adj)
angry with sb for doing sth (adj)
annoyed about sth (adj)
annoyed with sb for doing sth (adj)
answer to (n)
apologise to sb for sth (v)

apply for sth (v)
arrest sb for sth (v)
arrive at (a small place) (v)
arrive in (a town) (v)
ashamed of (adj)
ask for (v) (but: **ask sb a question**)
astonished at/by (adj)
attitude to/towards (n)
aware of (adj)

B

bad at (adj)
begin with (v)
believe in (v)
belong to (v)

blame sb for sth (v)
blame sth on sb (v)
(someone is) to blame for sth (v)
bored with (adj)

borrow sth from sb (v)
brilliant at (adj)
bump into (v)

C

capable of (adj)
care about (v)
care for sb/sth (v)
(take) care of (n)
cause of (n)
charge sb with (v)
cheque for (n)
clever of you to (adj)
close to (adj)

collide with (v)
communicate with (v)
complain to sb about sth/sb (v)
concentrate on (v)
concerned about sth (adj)
congratulate sb on sth (v)
connection between (n)
(but: **in connection with**)
conscious of (adj)

consist of (v)
contact between (n) (but: **in contact with**)
cope with (v)
crash into (v)
crowded with (adj)
cruel to (adj)
cure for (n)
cut into small pieces (v)

D

damage to (n)
decide on (v)
decrease in (n)
delighted with (adj)
demand for (n)
depend on (v)

die of (v)
die in an accident (v)
difference between (n)
different from/to (adj)
disadvantage of (n)
disappointed with (adj)

divide into (v)
do sth about (v)
dream about (v)
dream of (v) (= imagine)
drive into (v)
due to (phrasal prep)

E

engaged to sb (adj)
envious of (adj)

excellent at (adj)
excited about (adj)

explain sth to sb (v)

F

fall in (n)
famous for (adj)
fed up with (adj)
fight for (v)
fond of (adj)

forget about (v)
forgive sb for (v)
(un)friendly to (adj)
frightened of (adj)
full of (adj)

furious about sth (adj)
furious with sb for doing sth (adj)

G

generous of sb (to do sth) (adj)
generous to sb (adj)

glance at (v)
good at (adj)

(be) good to sb (adj)
good of sb (to do sth) (adj)

H

happen to (v)
hear about (v) (= be told)

hear from (v) (= receive a letter)
hear of (v) (= learn that sth or sb exists)

hopeless at (adj)

I

impressed by/with (adj)
incapable of (adj)
increase in (n)

insist on (v)
intelligent of sb (to do sth) (adj)
interested in (adj)

invitation to (n)
invite sb to (v)

J	jealous of (adj)		
K	keen on sth (adj) kind of sb (to do sth) (adj)	kind to (adj)	key to (n)
L	laugh at (v) leave for (v) listen to (v)	live on (v) look after (phr v) (= take care of) look at/have a look at (v)	look for (phr v) (= search for)
M	married to (adj)	mean of sb (to do sth) (adj)	mean to (adj)
N	need for (n)	nice of sb (to do sth) (adj)	nice to (adj)
O	optimistic about (adj)		
P	pay for (v) photograph of (n) picture of (n) (un)pleasant to (adj) pleased with (adj)	point at (v) (im)polite of sb (to do sth) (adj) (im)polite to (adj) popular with (adj) prefer sth to sth else (v)	prevent sb from (v) protect against/from (v) proud of (adj) provide sb with (v) put pressure on sb (exp)
R	reaction to (n) reason for (n) receive from (v) regard as (v) relationship between (n) (but: **a good relationship with sb**)	rely on (v) remind sb of/about (v) remind sb to do sth (v) reply to (n/v) responsible for (adj) rise in (n)	rude of sb (to do sth) (adj) rude to (adj) run into (phr v)
S	satisfied with (adj) save sb from (v) scared of (adj) search for (v/n) sensible of sb (to do sth) (adj) sentence sb to (v) shocked at/by (adj) short of (adj) shout at (v)	shout to sb (v) silly of sb to do sth (adj) similar to (adj) smile at (v) solution to (n) sorry about (adj) (= sorry for sb) sorry for doing sth (adj) speak to (v) spend money on sth (v)	spend time doing sth (v) split into (v) stare at (v) stupid of sb (to do sth) (adj) succeed in (v) suffer from (v) surprised at/by (adj) surrounded by (adj) suspicious of (adj)
T	talk to (v) terrified of (adj) think about/of (v)	throw at (v) throw to (v) tired of (adj)	top of sth (n) translate from ... into (v) turn sth into sth (phr v)
U	unreasonable of sb (to do sth) (adj)	upset about (adj)	
W	wait for (v) warn sb against/about/of (v)	warn sb not to do sth (v) worried about (adj)	write to sb (v)

At	at the bottom of at first	at least at the weekend	at 4, Rose St.
By	by accident by bus/train/plane/ helicopter/taxi/coach/ ship/boat/sea/air/car, etc. (but: **on a/the bus/plane/ train/coach/ship/boat in a taxi/car/helicopter/plane**)	by chance by cheque by mistake by post/airmail	by Rembrandt by Shakespeare by the time
For	for breakfast/lunch/dinner for a drink for fun (= for amusement)	for help (go to a place) for a holiday/my holiday(s)	for a swim for a walk for a while
From	from time to time from now on	from that day on	
In	in agony in an armchair in cash in the (city) centre in the/a city in common	in the countryside in disbelief in the distance in one's free time in the fresh air in a hurry	in love (with) in one's opinion in other words in power in time
Into	into pieces		
On	on business on the (west) coast on a(n) cruise/excursion/ trip/tour on a diet on an expedition	on a farm (but: **in a field**) on fire on the (4th) floor (of) on foot on the other hand on holiday	on page ... on the phone/telephone on the radio/TV on the right/left on strike on a trip
Out of	out of control	out of date	out of order
To	to one's relief	to one's horror	
Under	under control	under repair	under threat

1 Use the prepositions in the list below to complete the sentences.

for, of, to, from, in, about, with, into

1 Michael is terrified .....of..... flying and hasn't travelled by plane for ten years.
2 Mr Peters was responsible .... the accident and had to pay for all the repairs.
3 The lifeguard jumped into the pool and saved the little boy ...from.... drowning.
4 Mary apologised ....to.... Lucy for not being able to meet her for lunch.
5 John is interested ....in....... studying Law and is planning to attend a law school abroad.
6 "Excuse me. Could you please take a picture ......of...... me in front of Big Ben?" she asked.
7 I wonder how Sue is. I haven't heard ...from.. her since September.
8 Scientists who do research and find cures ...for.... diseases should be rewarded.
9 Melissa is very jealous ....of...... her little brother as he gets most of the attention.
10 A: Do you know where the post office is?
   B: Yes. It's close ....to..... the school.
11 They forgot ...about... their differences and became best friends once again.
12 A: Do you believe .... ghosts?
   B: Of course not. How ridiculous!
13 The train leaves .....from.. Luxembourg at 1:35.
14 The children woke up very early as they were excited .... going to the beach for the day.
15 "Did you hear that Don is getting married .... Rachel?" he asked.
16 He lost control of the car and drove ...into.. a tree.
17 There is a need ....of....... more parks in the city.
18 "Where have you been? I've been waiting for.. you since two o'clock," she said.
19 Maria was so pleased ...with.... her children's progress at school that she bought them a treat.
20 One of the things France is famous ...for... is its cuisine.

2 Underline the correct word(s).

1 How rude **of**/to Frank to use Penny's car without asking her.
2 Look **after**/**at** that rainbow. Isn't it beautiful!
3 It was very kind **to**/of Mark to drive us to the airport.
4 Paula had a bad dream **about**/of monsters last night.
5 The mayor arrived **in**/at New York an hour ago.

6 What's the difference **between**/from an ocean and a sea?
7 I'm calling in connection **between**/**with** your advertisement in the Carlton Times.
8 "Did you hear **of**/**about** Tim and Helen? They're getting married next summer," said Bill.
9 Mr Marcus is extremely generous **to**/**of** all his friends.
10 Unfortunately, Tanya didn't agree **to**/**with** cook for the party, so we'll have to hire a caterer.
11 My best friend almost died **in**/**of** a boating accident last year.
12 Stop shouting **at**/**to** me! I said I was sorry.
13 It is impolite **of**/**to** ask someone how much money they earn.
14 "I'm sorry **for**/**with** breaking your window, Mrs Donaldson," said Sam.
15 My sister was so angry that she threw a pillow **to**/**at** me.
16 Jonathan has invited all his friends **to**/**at** his birthday party next Saturday.
17 My father was furious **with**/**about** my brother for staying out so late.
18 The passengers were extremely angry **with**/**about** the cancellation of their flight.
19 Monica is a very sensitive person. She really cares **for**/**about** other people's feelings.
20 I was terribly annoyed **with**/**about** the hairdresser for cutting my hair so short.

3 Choose the correct item.

1 Joanne is so .... drawing that she has decided to study Art at university.
   A bad at   **B** upset about   **C** good at

2 Tommy was .... school yesterday because he had a temperature.
   A absent from   **B** worried about
   C satisfied with

3 It was very .... Larry to throw a surprise birthday party for Lauren.
   A nice of   **B** optimistic about
   C disappointed with

4 Who did the police .... robbing the corner shop?
   A charge with   **B** complain to   **C** warn about

5 .... the hurricane, all schools in the area were closed for three days.
   A According to   **B** Due to
   C In connection with

6 Amy saw an advertisement for a secretarial position and decided to .... it.
   A apply for   B aim at   C answer to

7 Mr Mattle was .... his new assistant as she was extremely impolite to the customers.
   A bored with   B furious with
   C satisfied with

8 The criminal was .... fifteen years in prison.
   A damaged to   B sentenced to   C agreed to

9 You shouldn't .... breaking your CD player.
   A apologise to Leslie   B rely on Leslie
   C blame Leslie for

10 We ate at a wonderful restaurant which is quite .... the locals.
   A keen on   B popular with   C nice to

4 Fill in the gaps with the correct preposition.

1 A: Do you know where the Johnsons live?
   B: Yes, they live ...at............ 102, Riley Road ......in.............. the city centre. I think their apartment is ...on........ the 6th floor.

2 A: Do you drive to work?
   B: No, I always go to work ...on......... foot but I return ....by...... taxi.

3 A: The Simms must be away ...on.... holiday. The lights in their house have been off for days.
   B: Didn't I tell you that they went ...on....... a cruise but that they will be back ...in...... time for our dinner party next week?

4 A: What do you like doing .... your free time?
   B: I love reading plays ...by..... Shakespeare and sometimes I go window-shopping ...in.... town.

5 A: How about going ...to for... a swim at... the weekend?
   B: I'd rather go ...for..... a walk ...in..... the countryside.

6 A: Did you know that Mary went to a dietician ...for...... help?
   B: Really?
   A: Yes. She was put ...on........ a diet and seems to have her weight .... control now.

7 A: When I was ...in........ the bus yesterday, I got really embarrassed.
   B: Why? What happened?
   A: I stepped on a woman's foot, ...by............. accident of course, and she started screaming at me.

8 A: I heard ...on..... the radio that the bank near here was robbed this morning.
   B: Oh really! I thought I heard sirens ...in....... the distance early this morning.

5 Use the prepositions in the list below to complete the sentences.

at, by, for, in, on, out of, from, into, to

1 Let's meet ...for.... a drink at O'Malley's on Friday night.

2 "Can I call you back tomorrow? I'm ...in........ a hurry right now and don't have time to talk to you," she said.

3 After the storm, all the telephones in my neighbourhood were ...in.... order and had to be repaired.

4 A: Can I speak to Mr Watley?
   B: I'm afraid Mr Watley is away ...on.... business. Would you like to leave a message?

5 ...To........ my horror, I noticed that the lock of the front door had been broken.

6 Customers can pay ...by........ cheque if they wish to.

7 A: I was half an hour late for my lesson this morning.
   B: Did you apologise ...to........ your teacher?

8 During the earthquake, one of my most expensive vases broke ...into.. a thousand pieces.

9 ...From... time to time she would stop whatever she was doing, look out of the window and day-dream.

10 A: Did you grow up in a city?
   B: No, I didn't. I spent most of my childhood ...on...... a farm.

Revision: Verbs, Adjectives, Nouns with Prepositions

6 Underline the correct preposition.

1 Jason accused Sam **of**/about breaking into his computer files.

2 If you're fed up for/**with** doing the housework, hire a cleaner.

3 A: What was Julie so upset at/**about** this morning?
   B: She almost had a car crash.

4 **To**/With our relief, we were evacuated from our home before the storm hit.

5 "Would you like to pay on/**in** cash or by credit card, Sir?" asked the shop assistant.

6 Kate succeeded to/**in** winning first prize for her science project on the solar system.

7   Mr Bradley complained to Carl's mother **about/for** her son's behaviour in class.

8   The local council have been trying to prevent people **from/of** dropping litter in the town's streets.

9   **In/At** first, I thought she was arrogant, but then I realised she was just shy.

10 He has been playing that computer game all day. He is bored **at/with** it, now.

11 Southern parts of the USA are constantly **under/ in** threat of hurricanes.

12 One of the main reasons **for/about** the hole in the ozone layer is air pollution.

13 A: Where are you going **for/at** your holidays this year?
    B: Nowhere. We're redecorating our house.

14 The audience was amazed **of/by** the magnificent voice of the opera singer.

15 "Can you please look at me when I'm talking **about/to** you?" she said.

16 Being an only child can have its advantages. **On/ In** the other hand, it can be lonely at times.

17 "Do you think she'll ever forgive me **for/of** telling Matt her secret?" Paul asked.

18 "Is the cheapest way to send a parcel to Australia **on/by** airmail?" he asked.

19 The employees got a rise because their boss was extremely satisfied **with/about** their work.

20 "Are you aware **about/of** the dangers of smoking?" said Sarah.

21 I have a very good relationship **for/with** my colleagues.

22 **At/By** the time they got to the cinema, the film had already started.

23 "Don't forget to return the books you borrowed **from/at** the public library," said Mum.

24 The children are very fond **with/of** chocolate biscuits.

25 I met Mr Harrods **in/by** chance in the lift.

26 There's a lot we can do to protect our rainforests **from/of** destruction.

27 The police arrested Mrs Davis **on/for** shoplifting.

28 She worked as a waitress **in/for** a while before going to university.

29 Spiders don't frighten me, but I'm really scared **with/of** snakes.

30 I dialled the wrong number **by/on** mistake.

31 The antique shop was full **with/of** old pieces of furniture.

32 My brother and I have very few things **on/in** common.

7   **Fill in the gaps with the correct preposition to complete the letter below.**

Dear Mum and Dad,

Hello from Amsterdam! Joe and I arrived 1) .... this fantastic city two days ago and I thought I'd write 2) .... you to tell you how great it is.

Yesterday, we went to the Van Gogh Museum and saw some amazing paintings 3) .... the artist. We were so impressed 4) .... his work that we stayed at the museum for six hours! We also took a bicycle ride through the peaceful streets and I was astonished 5) .... the beauty of the houses. In fact, they reminded me 6) .... home. I've taken lots of photographs 7) .... them so you can see for yourself.

This morning we met a very nice Dutch couple and they've invited us 8) .... have dinner with them tonight. They live 9) .... a houseboat so the evening should be fun. I just hope Joe doesn't fall 10) .... the canal — you know how clumsy he is!

Anyway, we're leaving 11) .... Paris tomorrow afternoon, so you'll hear 12) .... us again in a few days.

Lots of love,
Carol

8   **Match Column A to Column B.**

A	B
1 Does this red umbrella	a that I always order takeaway food.
2 It took Mr Parks a while to	b to congratulate me on the birth of my daughter.
3 The project aims at finding ways	c at the shopping centre this afternoon.
4 Being a doctor, one has to cope with	d get accustomed to the fact that he had retired.
5 It's time we did something about	e to help decrease noise pollution.
6 My parents prefer jazz music	f crime in our neighbourhood.
7 Can I rely on you	g belong to Chris?
8 We bumped into our French teacher	h working long hours.
9 My brother called me	i to classical music.
10 I'm so hopeless at cooking	j to have the order delivered by Tuesday?

Irregular Verbs

Infinitive	Past	Past Participle	Infinitive	Past	Past Participle
be	was	been	let	let	let
bear	bore	born(e)	lie	lay	lain
beat	beat	beaten	light	lit	lit
become	became	become	lose	lost	lost
begin	began	begun	make	made	made
bite	bit	bitten	mean	meant	meant
blow	blew	blown	meet	met	met
break	broke	broken	pay	paid	paid
bring	brought	brought	put	put	put
build	built	built	read	read	read
burn	burnt (burned)	burnt (burned)	ride	rode	ridden
burst	burst	burst	ring	rang	rung
buy	bought	bought	rise	rose	risen
can	could	(been able to)	run	ran	run
catch	caught	caught	say	said	said
choose	chose	chosen	see	saw	seen
come	came	come	seek	sought	sought
cost	cost	cost	sell	sold	sold
cut	cut	cut	send	sent	sent
deal	dealt	dealt	set	set	set
dig	dug	dug	sew	sewed	sewn
do	did	done	shake	shook	shaken
draw	drew	drawn	shine	shone	shone
dream	dreamt (dreamed)	dreamt (dreamed)	shoot	shot	shot
drink	drank	drunk	show	showed	shown
drive	drove	driven	shut	shut	shut
eat	ate	eaten	sing	sang	sung
fall	fell	fallen	sit	sat	sat
feed	fed	fed	sleep	slept	slept
feel	felt	felt	smell	smelt (smelled)	smelt (smelled)
fight	fought	fought	speak	spoke	spoken
find	found	found	spell	spelt (spelled)	spelt (spelled)
fly	flew	flown	spend	spent	spent
forbid	forbade	forbidden	spill	spilt	spilt
forget	forgot	forgotten	split	split	split
forgive	forgave	forgiven	spoil	spoilt (spoiled)	spoilt (spoiled)
freeze	froze	frozen	spread	spread	spread
get	got	got	spring	sprang	sprung
give	gave	given	stand	stood	stood
go	went	gone	steal	stole	stolen
grow	grew	grown	stick	stuck	stuck
hang	hung (hanged)	hung (hanged)	sting	stung	stung
have	had	had	strike	struck	struck
hear	heard	heard	swear	swore	sworn
hide	hid	hidden	sweep	swept	swept
hit	hit	hit	swim	swam	swum
hold	held	held	take	took	taken
hurt	hurt	hurt	teach	taught	taught
keep	kept	kept	tear	tore	torn
know	knew	known	tell	told	told
lay	laid	laid	think	thought	thought
lead	led	led	throw	threw	thrown
learn	learnt (learned)	learnt (learned)	understand	understood	understood
leave	left	left	wake	woke	woken
lend	lent	lent	wear	wore	worn
			win	won	won
			write	wrote	written

PROGRESS TESTS

NAME:..   DATE: ....

CLASS: ....   MARK: ....

(Time: 20 minutes)

Choose the correct item.

1 Although she has a car, she .... to work.
   A is walking   B walking   C walks

2 Julia is the chef .... cooks lunch every day.
   A who   B which   C whose

3 My baby brother .... with his toys at the moment.
   A had played   B was playing   C is playing

4 The house .... is over one hundred years old belongs to Mrs DuPont.
   A who   B which   C that

5 Fred is impatient .... rude.
   A also   B and   C but

6 1879 was the year .... Albert Einstein was born.
   A when   B which   C why

7 Your new outfit .... fabulous.
   A look   B looks   C is looking

8 .... was she writing a letter to this morning?
   A Which   B What   C Who

9 He took off his jumper .... he was hot.
   A because   B so   C and

10 A: Ellen loves spicy food.
   B: Yes, I know. She .... cooks Mexican dishes.
   A never   B seldom   C always

11 Dave .... about buying a new CD player.
   A is thinking   B thinks   C thinking

12 That's the boy .... got a blue and red bicycle.
   A who   B whose   C who's

13 I love reading .... I hate watching TV.
   A but   B also   C and

14 That's the girl .... mother is a singer.
   A whose   B which   C who

15 Eddie doesn't mind going to bed late, but he .... waking up early in the morning.
   A disliked   B disliking   C dislikes

16 I heard a joke today .... was very funny.
   A which   B who   C whom

17 A: Does Jake work at the weekend?
   B: No, he ....
   A doesn't   B do   C does

18 The shop .... I bought my jacket from is closing down.
   A whose   B which   C where

19 A: Does Mr Harvey mow the lawn every Saturday?
   B: Yes, he .... does.
   A never   B always   C rarely

20 Do you know .... Al didn't come on the picnic?
   A which   B where   C why

NAME:... DATE: ....

CLASS: .... MARK: ....

(Time: 20 minutes)

Choose the correct item.

1 A: What time .... you leave school yesterday?
   B: At four o'clock.
   A have   B does   **C** did

2 I love reading .... *Guardian* newspaper every Sunday morning.
   A the   B a   C an

3 At half past six last night we .... dinner.
   A are having   **B** were having C have

4 The food was .... spicy I couldn't eat it.
   A so   B such   C such a

5 A: Where's Bill?
   B: He's .... to the basketball game.
   A been going   B been   **C** gone

6 It was .... difficult crossword puzzle that I couldn't finish it.
   A such a   B so   C such

7 A: Is Lesley at home?
   B: Yes, she's .... arrived.
   A just   B since   C already

8 Many different languages are spoken in .... Europe.
   A the   **B** —   C an

9 A: Why is Paul tired?
   B: Well, he .... in the library for hours!
   A is studying   **B** has been studying
   C has studied

10 It was .... boring lecture that I left before it was over.
   A such a   B so   C such

11 I've only .... to the opera once.
   A been   B been going C gone

12 A: Would you like a cup of .... coffee?
   B: No, thanks.
   A a   B the   **C** —

13 They .... the airport as soon as they had collected their luggage.
   A left   B leave   C are leaving

14 His costume was .... original that he won first prize.
   A so   B such a   C such

15 She has .... in her studio since six o'clock this morning.
   A been painting   **B** painted   C paint

16 Our teacher told us all about .... Second World War today.
   A the   B which   C a

17 Karen .... a hairdresser for two years.
   A has been   B was being C is being

18 There were .... cars in the street that we couldn't find a parking space.
   A such   **B** so many   C such many

19 The baby hasn't been sleeping well ....
   A yet   B since   **C** lately

20 Do you remember meeting .... Carl's grandfather?
   A the   **B** —   C a

NAME: .... DATE: ....

CLASS: .... MARK: ....

(Time: 20 minutes)

Choose the correct item.

1 Molly used to .... watching cartoons when she was young.
A loving B loved C love

2 First, he had dinner, then he .... the newspaper.
A read B was reading C had read

3 The Rosens .... abroad for fifteen years before they moved back to England.
A lived B have lived C were living

4 Peter was listening to his favourite CD when Paul ....
A came in B was coming in
C had come in

5 You .... chew gum in class.
A must B mustn't C needn't

6 I think History is less interesting .... Geography.
A from B of C than

7 Valerie was making the beds while Mark .... the floor.
A was sweeping B swept C had swept

8 You .... have a driving licence in order to drive a car.
A mustn't B needn't C must

9 Brian isn't as .... as Richard.
A friendly B friendlier C friendliest

10 My grandfather often .... old films.
A has watched B watches
C had been watching

11 Maria entered the room very quietly .... she didn't want to wake anyone up.
A while B so C as

12 You .... feed the dog. I fed it this morning.
A needn't B need C must

13 Mary .... the house by the time it started to rain.
A reached B had reached
C was reaching

14 George never .... eat vegetables when he was a teenager.
A didn't use to B uses to C used to

15 I .... the ambulance siren wailing as I was walking through the city centre.
A heard B was hearing
C had been hearing

16 A: Is Jessica .... than Susie?
B: No, I don't think so.
A talented B as talented
C more talented

17 Had you .... to San Francisco before?
A been B went C go

18 You .... make an appointment to see a doctor. The clinic is open 24 hours a day.
A need B needn't C mustn't

19 She .... a book all night and was very sleepy the next morning.
A is reading B had been reading
C was reading

20 Rachel was watering the plants while her children .... in the garden.
A was playing B were playing
C play

125

NAME: ....   DATE: ....

CLASS: ....   MARK: ....

(Time: 20 minutes)

Choose the correct item.

1   She .... her leg so she couldn't go water-skiing.
   A was breaking   **B** had broken   **C** broken

2   I hope Tracey .... home soon.
   A has been coming   **B** will come   **C** is coming

3   Did they .... travel a lot when they were first married?
   A using to   **B** used to   **C** use to

4   If they .... up early, I'll make them a big breakfast.
   A woke   **B** are waking   **C** wake

5   He called a taxi .... he had finished packing.
   A as soon as   **B** while   **C** by

6   We .... to spend the afternoon relaxing in the garden.
   A will   **B** are going   **C** going

7   A: Sorry I'm late.
   B: You should be! I .... for over an hour.
   A am waiting   **B** have been waiting
   C wait

8   If your father comes home now, we .... a pizza for dinner.
   A are ordering   **B** order   **C** will order

9   They .... a table before they went to the restaurant.
   A are reserving   **B** had reserved
   C were reserving

10   You may .... my camera if you promise to return it tomorrow.
   A to use   **B** used   **C** use

11   I .... my lawyer on Monday.
   A seen   **B** am seeing   **C** see

12   She turns on the answering machine every morning before she .... for work.
   A leaves   **B** has left   **C** is leaving

13   I'm afraid I .... late for dinner this evening.
   A will be   **B** can be   **C** am

14   A: Have you lived alone before?
   B: No, but I'm .... to it.
   A getting used   **B** used   **C** was used

15   If I .... work early tonight, I'll give you a ring.
   A will finish   **B** finish   **C** finished

16   We .... for an hour before we found the perfect picnic spot.
   A had been driving   **B** have been driving
   C were driven

17   A: I've got a high temperature.
   B: I .... you an aspirin.
   A going to get   **B** get   **C** will get

18   Joan and Tim had their first baby five years ....
   A since   **B** ago   **C** before

19   A: Where .... going for your birthday?
   B: To *La Mama's*.
   A do you   **B** are you   **C** will you

20   By the time she .... to the bus station, the bus had already left.
   A was getting   **B** gets   **C** got

NAME:... DATE:.....................................

CLASS:... MARK:....................................

(Time: 20 minutes)

Choose the correct item.

1 This time next Sunday I .... at my friend's party.
   A will dance   **B will be dancing**
   C am dancing

2 He said that he .... call me the next day.
   A will   **B would**   C is going to

3 He asked me if Susie .... reading his book.
   A had finished   B was finished C finish

4 Mrs Simmons .... the report by Tuesday.
   A will be writing   B is writing
   C will have written

5 She refused .... him a pair of jeans.
   A to buy   B buy   **C buying**

6 Robert .... me that Janet was sleeping.
   A said   **B told**   C says

7 Watching too much TV causes us to become inactive. ...., people who watch a lot of television may become antisocial.
   A But   B However   **C Moreover**

8 More and more people .... computers in the future.
   A have used   **B will be using**
   C are getting used

9 Amanda suggested .... to the theatre on Friday night.
   A going   B having gone C go

10 Jean hopes she .... herself a car by the time she is thirty years old.
    A will be buying   **B will have bought**
    C will buy

11 Georgia apologised for .... so rude to her mother.
    A having been   B have been   C been

12 He said that he .... hungry and was going to make himself a sandwich.
    A was   B had been   C has been

13 A: What did Alison say?
    B: She said that she .... pick up the children on her way home.
    A has   **B would**   C was

14 I will have done all my homework before we .... out tonight.
    A go   B will go   C are going

15 Bob .... the TV until next weekend.
    A will repair   **B won't have repaired**
    C will be repaired

16 My doctor advised me .... swimming.
    A to taking up   B take up   **C to take up**

17 I want you to .... me the truth!
    A say to   **B tell**   C say

18 .... living in a big city is exciting, it can be tiring and stressful to travel from one part of the city to another.
    A Although   B However   C Moreover

19 Who was this letter written ....?
    A from   **B by**   C with

20 My teacher told us that the telephone .... by Alexander Graham Bell.
    A was invented   B is invented
    C have been invented

NAME:.. DATE: ....

CLASS: .... MARK: ....

(Time: 20 minutes)

Choose the correct item.

1 She offered to .... the children to the cottage for the weekend.
A took   B take   C taking

2 A suspicious-looking man .... running away from the scene of the crime.
A was seen   B is seeing   C is seen

3 She .... me of telling everybody her secret.
A is being accused   B accused   C accuse

4 The baby's skin .... very soft.
A feels   B feel   C is feeling

5 He complained that I always .... too much money.
A spending   B spends   C spend

6 The salad was made .... lettuce, onions and cucumber.
A of   B by   C with

7 He asked us not .... late for the meeting.
A be   B to be   C being

8 We .... allowed to stay up till midnight last Friday.
A were   B will be   C had

9 I .... them to go sailing with us this summer.
A invite   B inviting   C invited

10 Pat suggested .... to the cinema on Saturday.
A going   B go   C to go

11 The curtains .... by Marie.
A are making   B are being made
C made

12 He ordered us ....
A not to move   B to not move   C not move

13 I work .... a photographer for *Elegance* magazine.
A such   B like   C as

14 The pool must be .... on Sunday.
A cleans   B cleaning   C cleaned

15 He took the knife away from the child and .... that it was dangerous.
A explained   B explaining   C explains

16 Their kitten was rescued .... their neighbour.
A of   B with   C by

17 She .... to throw their toys in the bin if they didn't put them away.
A is threatening   B threatened
C threatens

18 The flowers would have been .... in the garden by now if I hadn't been so busy lately.
A planting   B plants   C planted

19 She denied that she .... the suspect.
A knew   B is knowing   C was known

20 Although Tina is only three years old, she swims .... a fish.
A like   B as   C such

NAME:... DATE:...

CLASS:.. MARK:...

(Time: 20 minutes)

Choose the correct item.

1 Jack wishes he .... with his brother.
   A is fighting   B would have fought
   C hadn't fought

2 The silver candlestick needs ....
   A polishing   B to polishing C polish

3 Carl is expected .... the gold medal.
   A win   B to win   C to winning

4 If I were you, I .... how to drive a car.
   A would learn   B will learn
   C would learning

5 If only I .... where he works.
   A knew   B have known C know

6 If we had called the travel agent earlier, we
   .... tickets to Toronto.
   A have got   B could get
   C would have got

7 If my typewriter worked, I .... your report
   for you.
   A would type   B would typing C will type

8 If Donna .... earlier at the party, she would
   have seen Billy.
   A arrived   B had arrived C arrives

9 I wish I .... nearer to my office so I wouldn't
   have to get up so early.
   A had lived   B live   C lived

10 The flowers for the reception need to ....
   A be ordered   B be ordering C ordering

11 Dr Matthews .... to have saved many
   people during the war.
   A is being known   B is known   C has known

12 If Mary worked harder, she .... a promotion.
   A will be getting   B will get   C would get

13 We had a great time in Mexico, ... the bad
   weather.
   A although   B in spite   C despite

14 If Joe .... to Hollywood, he would have
   been a film star.
   A had gone   B went   C goes

15 New chairs .... to be bought for the office.
   A are needing   B needs   C need

16 It .... that a student broke into the school
   library late last night.
   A is believed   B has been believed
   C was believed

17 What would you do if your car .... in the
   middle of nowhere?
   A broken down   B broke down
   C breaks down

18 .... studying very hard for her exam, she
   still didn't pass it.
   A Nevertheless   B Although   C In spite of

19 I wish I .... the flu.
   A wasn't having   B haven't had C didn't have

20 If only I .... how to get in touch with her!
   A have known   B knew   C will know

NAME:... DATE:...

CLASS:.. MARK:...

(Time: 20 minutes)

Choose the correct item.

1 "Excuse me. Can you .... me with my bags, please?"
A to help   B helping   **C** help

2 She works at the library, ...?
A doesn't she   B isn't she   C didn't she

3 My brother refused .... me use his car this weekend.
A let   **B** to let   C letting

4 Emily taught .... how to play the violin.
A itself   B himself   **C** herself

5 I don't remember .... the alarm system this morning.
A turning on   B to turn on   C turn on

6 Tom isn't going to the theatre, ...?
A does he   B was he   **C** is he

7 Try .... to someone. I'm sure it will make you feel better.
A talking   B talk   C to talking

8 Don't call me at the office, ...?
A do you   **B** won't you   C will you

9 She made him .... the garage.
A cleaning   B clean   **C** to clean

10 Ed hasn't got any brothers or sisters, ...?
A does he   B isn't he   **C** has he

11 I really regret .... my car.
A selling   B to sell   C sell

12 You have to learn to relax ....
A itself   **B** –   C yourself

13 John and I can't agree on where .... for our holidays.
A go   B going   **C** to go

14 Let's go for a walk, ...?
A won't we   **B** shall we   C will we

15 I saw her .... the road.
A cross   **B** to cross   C to crossing

16 Ben injured .... on a skiing trip.
A itself   B him   **C** himself

17 It's no use .... the toaster. We need to buy a new one.
A fixing   B to fix   C fix

18 I am clever, ...?
A was I   **B** aren't I   C are I

19 He stopped .... because his back hurt.
A exercise   B to exercise   **C** exercising

20 They rarely go out any more, ...?
A do they   B does they   C didn't they

NAME: ....   DATE: ....

CLASS: ....   MARK: ....

(Time: 20 minutes)

Choose the correct item.

1 I'm going to the supermarket .... some milk and eggs.
   A to getting   **B** to get   C get

2 He's .... to reach the top shelf.
   A tall enough   B enough tall   C too tall

3 The .... were playing basketball in the park.
   A childs   **B** children   C child

4 Annie and Stacy were .... to be admitted into the cinema without an adult.
   A young enough   B young   C too young

5 .... the storm, the meeting was cancelled.
   A Due to fact that   B Because   **C** Due to

6 Tim is taking driving lessons so that he .... pass his driving test and get a licence.
   A could   B would   **C** can

7 Both my brothers .... in Athens, Georgia.
   A live   B lives   C is living

8 The cake was .... delicious that we ate it all.
   A so   B such   C too

9 All the girls in my class .... dance lessons this year.
   A taking   **B** are taking   C take

10 It was .... beautiful dress that I bought it.
    A such   **B** such a   C so

11 Elizabeth is .... to own a mansion.
    A rich enough   B too rich   C rich

12 They booked a room in a hotel by the sea so that they .... go swimming every day.
    A could   B can   C may

13 She set the timer on the oven .... she wouldn't burn the dinner.
    A in order to   **B** so that   C to

14 The police .... the area for clues.
    A is searching   B searches
    C are searching

15 He left work early .... not to be late for his doctor's appointment.
    A in order   B so that   C to

16 I drank a bottle of water .... I was extremely thirsty.
    A due to   **B** because   C because of

17 We had .... bad weather during our holiday that we left three days early.
    A so   B such a   **C** such

18 Many .... saw the accident and were able to explain what happened.
    A passer-bys   B passers-bys   **C** passers-by

19 .... there was a snowstorm last night, all schools are closed today.
    A Due to   **B** Due to the fact that
    C Because of

20 She moved to the countryside .... she wanted to live in a more peaceful area.
    A because of   B so   **C** as

NAME: ....

DATE: ....

CLASS: ....

MARK: ....

(Time: 20 minutes)

Choose the correct item.

1 He .... a doctor. He didn't go to medical school.
   A must be   **B** might be   **C** can't be

2 Don't call Sandy. It's midnight and she .... sleeping.
   A may be   **B** can't be   **C** may not be

3 To make a club sandwich you need three .... of bread.
   A slices   **B** bars   **C** pieces

4 There was .... in the cinema other than us.
   A no one   **B** anyone   **C** someone

5 How .... flour do you need for the sponge cake?
   A many   **B** any   **C** much

6 Is there .... I can do to help you?
   A someone   **B** nothing   **C** anything

7 Mark told me the .... joke I have ever heard.
   A funnier   **B** funniest   **C** funny

8 I .... go to the beach than to the mountains.
   A would rather   **B** would prefer   **C** prefer

9 Maria is taller .... Martha.
   A of   **B** than   **C** from

10 Bob is the tallest basketball player .... the team.
   A of   **B** in   **C** than

11 I've got .... apples. I think I'll make an apple pie.
   A few   **B** a few   **C** a little

12 I can hear .... knocking on the door.
   A anyone   **B** no one   **C** someone

13 George works as .... as Mike.
   A hard   **B** harder   **C** hardest

14 Michelle would prefer .... dinner rather than eat at a restaurant.
   A cook   **B** to cook   **C** cooking

15 Can I have .... grated cheese on my spaghetti, please?
   A a few   **B** little   **C** a little

16 They .... skiing. They don't know how to ski.
   A must be   **B** must have gone   **C** can't have gone

17 There is .... in the office today. It's Sunday.
   A nobody   **B** anybody   **C** somebody

18 The news .... on at 8:00 on Channel 4.
   A is   **B** are   **C** be

19 The children are laughing. They .... happy.
   A can't be   **B** might have been   **C** must be

20 New York is the most exciting city .... the USA.
   A in   **B** of   **C** at

NAME: .... DATE: ....

CLASS: .... MARK: ....

(Time: 20 minutes)

Choose the correct item.

1 He was .... after working the night shift.
   A exhausted   B exhausting
   C being exhausted

2 She had her car .... by a mechanic.
   A been serviced   B servicing   C serviced

3 We'd rather .... to the theatre last night.
   A go   B have gone   C have been

4 The Thomsons .... their house destroyed by a hurricane last summer.
   A has   B have   C had

5 A: I love jogging in the park early in the morning.
   B: .... I.
   A So do   B Nor did   C So did

6 Tony has his letters .... by his secretary.
   A types   B typing   C typed

7 I prefer working in the garden rather than .... the house.
   A cleaning   B cleans   C to clean

8 Alison will have her costume .... by her mother.
   A made   B make   C making

9 I'd rather you .... me first before you took my jacket.
   A had asked   B have asked   C asked

10 They must have their report .... by tomorrow.
   A writing   B written   C write

11 A: I won't go to Beth's party because it's too far away.
   B: .... I.
   A So will   B Nor will   C Nor do

12 He .... his windows cleaned when I arrived.
   A will have   B is having   C was having

13 She'd prefer to own a house .... own a flat.
   A rather than   B from   C than

14 She is having her dress .... by a famous French designer.
   A designed   B designing   C designs

15 Jerry is an extremely .... person.
   A amuse   B amused   C amusing

16 They didn't have their telephone .... until last Thursday.
   A repaired   B repairs   C to repair

17 A: I hate swimming in the sea.
   B: .... I.
   A Nor did   B So do   C Neither do

18 How often do you have your curtains ....?
   A clean   B cleaned   C cleaning

19 I'd rather you .... the ironing tonight.
   A did   B doing   C done

20 .... Mrs Phillips have her hair styled for the wedding?
   A Does   B Will   C Has

Phrasal Verbs & Prepositions

NAME: .... DATE: ....

CLASS: .... MARK: ....

(Time: 20 minutes)

Choose the correct item.

1 My little brother was born .... Christmas Day.
   A in   B on   C at

2 We ran .... paper at the office and had to order some more.
   A after   B out of   C over

3 "Mum, can you drive me to work tomorrow? The buses are .... strike".
   A on   B in   C at

4 It was extremely generous .... you to let us use your cottage last weekend.
   A to   B in   C of

5 Due to the heavy rainstorms, the football game was .... until next Saturday.
   A broken up   B turned down   C put off

6 Larry's father waited for him .... the school.
   A outside   B past   C towards

7 I .... some old pictures of my parents when I was cleaning the basement.
   A run into   B came across   C looked up

8 Mr Smith's toy shop is on Highland Avenue .... the supermarket and the bakery.
   A between   B against   C along

9 It was rude .... Julie not to call me to tell me she wasn't coming over for dinner.
   A of   B to   C from

10 Let's .... the TV. I think there's a good film on tonight.
   A put up   B turn into   C turn on

11 Why don't we meet for lunch .... noon?
   A on   B at   C in

12 The cat was hiding .... the bed.
   A over   B under   C down

13 The government provided the victims of the flood .... food and shelter.
   A by   B about   C with

14 The firefighter ran .... the burning house to save the young child.
   A into   B across   C among

15 Michelle is graduating from university .... this spring.
   A at   B ⌐   C in

16 Would you like to pay .... cash or by cheque?
   A in   B by   C with

17 The burglars ran out of the bank only to find themselves surrounded .... the police.
   A from   B by   C among

18 I'm going to collect the children from the park .... the afternoon.
   A in   B at   C by

19 After having a discussion for more than four hours, the executives still couldn't find a solution .... the problem.
   A with   B of   C to

20 The Blackstones are not .... from Hawaii until next week.
   A coming round   B coming back   C turning up